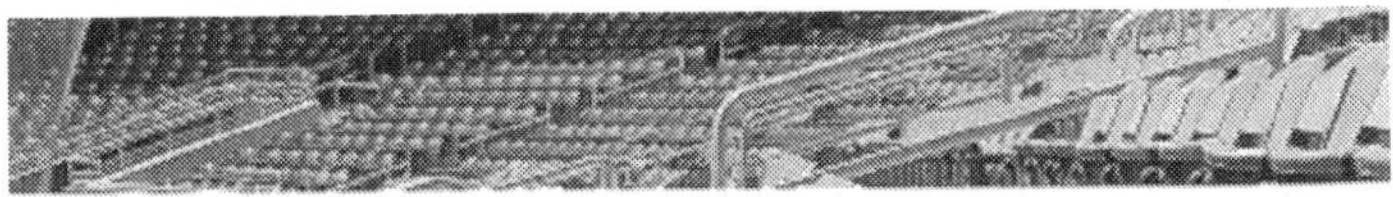

A View From My Seat

My baseball season with the Jumbo Shrimp

A View From My Seat

My baseball season with the Jumbo Shrimp

Armand Rosamilia

Rymfire Books

http://armandrosamilia.com

First Edition April 2018

Special thanks

to the Jacksonville Jumbo Shrimp staff and players, who were gracious enough during a pennant chase to sit down for a few minutes with me and answer my questions:

Randy Ready, Storm Davis, Braxton Lee, Austin Dean, Dustin Geiger, Joe Gunkel, Tyler Higgins, John Norwood, Alex Yarbrough, K.C. Serna, Ken Babby, Noel Blaha, Harold Craw, Chase Foster, Clayton Edwards, Linda McNabb, Brennan Earley, Andrea Williams, Roger Hoover, Marco LaNave, David Ratz, Ernest Hopkins and Ken Sparks

Also mom and dad

Always Shelly

Chapter 1: For The Love Of Baseball

I never played organized baseball in the Major Leagues. Never in college or high school. Not even in Little League or T-ball.

I did, however, hit homers like Jim Rice in my yard and on the street. I threw fastballs like Tom Seaver up at the elementary school with my friends during the summer. I fielded grounders like Jerry Remy in random dirt lots all over Belford and Middletown New Jersey as a kid.

Baseball was truly my first love. Even before reading, writing, heavy metal and the opposite sex, there was baseball. On TV in our living room, snuggled up with my dad between my brother and me watching the dreaded Yankees or the Mets on a lazy Saturday. At games not only in nearby Queens or the Bronx but in faraway places like Detroit, Baltimore and glorious Boston.

It wasn't until years later I realized not every family went through the same arguments and the passion about baseball like the Rosamilia family on Orchard Avenue.

I grew up a Red Sox fan. Rice and Yaz and Boggs and Clemens. More on the reasons later. My dad was a diehard Detroit Tigers fan. Al Kaline as a kid and Mark Fidrych when I was a kid. My brother inherited his love of the Yankees from my mother. She was a Thurman Munson fan, my brother loved Bucky Dent and Mike Pagliarulo.

We still talk baseball. Some would argue too much. My dad will call me during the day and immediately start talking about the latest trade or rumored trade. I might be waist-deep in a writing deadline but there is always time to talk baseball and about our teams.

It is still a ritual dating back to when I finally moved out of my parent's house and had my own place that we'll call one another when our team is eliminated from playoff contention.

There is no congratulating one another when their team wins. There is only sarcasm and loving their team lost, even if your own team was out of it weeks ago.

I sat down with my parents to interview them briefly about this book and our shared love of baseball.

I could've simply transcribed the hours of conversation we had that day and called it a book. They touched on baseball family lore I'd forgotten about or never knew.

And, of course, we chided one another about lost seasons and huge defeats. Even trying to have a civil conversation led to some arguments.

The arguments were epic.

"We were driving home from Cooperstown and we were stopped at a light. A guy pulled up next to us. Your father had his Tigers hat on, I had my Yankees

hat on and so did your brother. You were wearing your Red Sox hat. He rolled down the window and said we must have some great baseball seasons in our house. That was back when all three of our teams were all in the American League East division. I told him during the baseball season we hated each other," my mother told me.

As a kid I figured all families took a trip to Cooperstown to see the Baseball Hall of Fame. Why wouldn't you go?

It was my brother's birthday in July. We were in Cooperstown the week before the Hall of Fame weekend was happening. It was a year or so after Thurman Munson had died and there was a display at the Hall of Fame for him. It was a lot of Yankees when you walked in.

"It was ridiculous with all the Yankees stuff," my dad said with a smirk.

We'd do a lot of weekend trips if my dad wasn't working. Down to Seaside Heights or into Pennsylvania. My dad was collecting baseball cards so we'd find places he could buy them. I wasn't into it too much other than when he would bring packs home to open. I was way more into comic books as a kid. In 1978 at Wasserman's we'd buy the clear packs of Topps cards where you could see the three on top and read the names of the three on the bottom. Almost every weekend we'd head down to Englishtown, a huge outdoor flea market. Collingswood flea market. I'd buy comic books and dad would buy baseball cards.

I always assumed everyone was a baseball fan. All around the country, since everyone I grew up with and knew followed baseball. You followed MLB and the NFL in the Northeast. Most people watched the NBA and diehards watched the NHL. We watched the pro teams. It wasn't until I moved to Florida in my thirties that I realized how huge college football was and how many people watched NASCAR. I'm not a fan of either.

I'd followed minor league baseball. I'd been to quite a few games but it was mostly based around if the Red Sox were playing.

The years the Trenton Thunder were a Red Sox affiliate (1995 through 2002) as a Double-A team in the Eastern League I went to a couple of games every year until I moved to Florida in 2001. The drive became a hassle from where I grew up and maneuvering through Trenton wasn't fun anymore. I also had young kids who I couldn't take to a game with ease.

I didn't follow any minor league team. I was busy rooting for the Bosox.

Even when I moved to Florida and lived about twenty minutes from the Daytona Cubs, the Single-A Advanced member of the Florida State League, I only attended a handful of games after the initial excitement of having something to do.

I remember an ex knowing the groundskeeper for the Houston Astros and going to Kissimmee for a spring training game. I got to take my father. They might have been playing the Tigers, too.

The Gulf Coast League Braves play their home games at the Disney Wide World of Sports Complex and I took my son to a couple of games during the week. I remember we were the only two people sitting down the first base line. After him running to collect a dozen foul balls I told him to let someone else get one.

There wasn't anyone else around that day, although the next game we went to was on a weekend and the stadium was packed.

I remember driving from Daytona to Sarasota to see the last game of the Sarasota Red Sox in 2004. Part of the Southern League, they changed affiliations to the Reds the following year.

I took my son to see the Red Sox against the Tampa Bay Rays, too. There were more Red Sox fans than Rays fans in the stands, although it wasn't close to being a capacity crowd.

Unfortunately, none of my three kids inherited my love of baseball. My youngest, Katelynn, went to quite a few games with us in 2017 but she's mostly there for the crowd and the food, although Brian Anderson and Alex Yarbrough caught her teenage attention as well.

I'd been in Florida for fifteen years and only attended a handful of baseball games.

That would change when I discovered Jacksonville had their own Double-A baseball team and it was a fifteen minute drive to get there.

Chapter 2: Suns To Jumbo Shrimp

I still watched the Red Sox on TV every chance I had. I had bookmarked half a dozen baseball sites to get the latest news on my team. While I'd follow along to see what the rest of baseball was doing, the focus was always on my team.

And what the hated Yankees were doing.

I married Shelly Boyette in April 2015. We took a weeklong honeymoon cruise. No technology. No phone or internet. No baseball. It might have been the only week I didn't pay attention to the Red Sox and didn't care.

She was born and raised in Jacksonville. When we married I moved from near Daytona Beach to Jacksonville. Shelly wasn't from a sport's family. They didn't argue about which team was better. They didn't plan their weekends around what game was on TV.

Odd, to say the least.

She never watched baseball until she met me, and even then it was me watching the Red Sox and her doing something else. Playing Facebook games. Reading. Anything but paying attention to the game on TV.

Then she slowly started paying attention. She recognized Dustin Pedroia. She stopped whatever she was doing when Big Papi was batting. Shelly reluctantly and slowly became a baseball fan.

She began to see it wasn't a slow, boring game. There was strategy involved on both ends. My passion for the game and the Red Sox started rubbing off.

Then the Jacksonville Suns came onto my radar.

I'll let my wife tell you the rest of this. Not the entire book but maybe this chapter.

"I've lived in Jacksonville forever. About ten or twelve years ago I worked with a local youth group. We did an outing to see the Suns. Honestly, it was horribly boring. I was never a baseball fan. I think the next game I went to was last year. I'd forgotten about the Suns. I heard about them every once in awhile but I didn't follow sports. Besides the Suns game I'd only been to one more baseball game in my life: I saw the Atlanta Braves about twenty-five years ago. Again, I remember being bored out of my mind at that game, too. I had gone with people who didn't know baseball and didn't follow it," Shelly said.

I asked her why she'd ever gone back if she didn't have a pleasant experience watching baseball, a foreign concept to me. *"I had an outing for work and I was invited. We got to sit in the Hot Corner and it was the first time I actually had fun at a baseball game. We sat in great seats and the food was great and you love baseball so you answered my questions and were really into the game. It made it more interesting to me. I'd been watching baseball at home with you since we'd met and I could follow along but*

I wasn't really a fan. After that I was looking for something for my tenants for work. I usually do stuff in appreciation of them. I used to do cookouts or food but as we've grown it became unrealistic to coordinate it properly. I needed to find another way to thank them without breaking the bank. I figured sporting events would work. First I looked at football. I did it one year but it was expensive and I only had seven games worth of tickets since the Jaguars played one of their home games in London that year. I have over forty tenants. It didn't make sense. Around this time you wanted to go to another baseball game and I thought about how much fun we'd had. I ended up taking my office to a Suns game and we had an amazing time. Since having an outing wasn't expensive and everyone loved it, I thought my tenants might love it, too. Plus a full season would be seventy home games instead of seven and it would give me a chance to give away tickets to all my tenants. It was halfway through the season so I purchased the second half. Four tickets in a really good spot. Section 105. The tenants loved it. When we called them they jumped at the tickets. Then we got invited to a season ticket holder event at the end of the season. We ended up going to four or five games in 2016. I enjoyed going to all of them. In 2017 I bought the four seats for my tenants again since it was such a hit."

Don't let Shelly know, but seeing how much fun she was having at the games and how we could now talk about players and the game itself, I fell even more in love with this woman. As if that were possible. Seriously, I was looking forward to another season of watching baseball on TV and in person with her.

When did we decide to get our own season tickets?

"When the team reached out about renewing the seats for the tenants and explain the name change, we had already talked about how much you enjoyed going to the baseball games. I said I'd go if you wanted to. When I looked at the options I saw you could do specific games. Weekend games. Friday night tickets. There was a flex plan where you could buy a certain number of tickets and use them through the season. When I came to you and mentioned these plans you got all involved in it and wanted to go to all the games. We decided for the 2017 season we'd go all in. Try it out and see if it was too many games, especially for me, and then after that decide if we'd keep going or slow down. We ended up going to almost every game. It was a lot of fun. I already know we're going to buy season tickets for 2018, too. Being a season ticket holder is so worth it, not only for the deep discount on the price of tickets but because of the perks. People who work for the Jumbo Shrimp get to know us. We get invited to events for the season ticket holders. Getting into the game early. Getting to be the first in line for giveaways. As long as we're there half an hour before the gates officially open we are guaranteed a bobblehead or a backpack or a Shrimp neck pillow. Plus we know where we're sitting every night. And if the team makes the playoffs you get first dib on your seat, too. I think you missed five games and that was only because we were traveling. I might have missed nine or ten because of work,

especially the few day games during the week. We definitely got our money's worth out of it."

How did we pick those seats?

"We looked at the company seats, where we'd sat once or twice the previous season. We didn't like the netting in front of us. While it was great for the tenants and I'd have peace of mind no one was going to get scared over a foul ball coming back at them, we wanted no obstruction. To be honest, I also didn't want to sit right next to where the tenants were sitting. I didn't want to spend the game talking work and I knew you'd be bored with it, too. I didn't want the tenants to feel like they had to talk about work with me or act a certain way. I want people to go and relax and enjoy the game. I wanted to do the same thing. We moved three sections over, right behind the corner of the Jumbo Shrimp dugout. Four rows back on the end. Perfect seats for us. We also liked being on the home team side to see the players. In 2017 the company tickets moved up two rows but stayed in that section."

The last game of 2016 we went and spent a lot of money on Suns merchandise.

"Oh, yeah. We were excited because we knew we were going to get season tickets. I was definitely becoming a baseball fan. Our daughter was with us the last game of the season, too. We went to the gift shop. We bought a bunch of hats. A coffee mug. Shirts. We were ready for 2017 with all of our Suns gear. We go two months and then they make the announcement."

Name change.

"I had the same reaction as everyone else: what's Jumbo Shrimp have to do with Jacksonville? Clayton, our account executive, always called and said 'Hi, this is Clayton from the Suns' but then he called and said 'Hi, this is Clayton with the Jumbo Shrimp' and I said simply: why, Clayton? Why? He laughed and said he'd been hearing it all day. He went on to explain to me the guy who bought the Suns wanted to change the name to something fun to reenergize the ball team and the city. I still didn't see why Jumbo Shrimp was the new name. The reason he gave me: Jacksonville is a big city (Jumbo) but with a small town feel (Shrimp). Despite the woman in front of us at a game telling her friends the name is because Jacksonville is the shrimp capital of the world, which I don't believe is accurate, this was the reasoning behind the name change. At first I didn't like the name. They've been the Suns forever to me. As the season progressed I started liking the name and the logo more and more. I'm now all decked out in my Jumbo Shrimp gear."

It never bothered me at all because I understood minor league baseball and funky names of teams.

"For those of us who aren't huge baseball fans it was too goofy. It was great for the team. Attendance was huge. The turnout to games was awesome. The baseball Grounds were packed, especially the weekend games. But the Suns have been the Suns for as long as I can remember. Not that I had any attachment to them or cared, but they were always the Suns. When they changed the name I did what so many other locals did who never really went to games or followed the team and I got territorial about not

wanting them to change it. I look back and it didn't make sense but at the time it was the knee-jerk reaction. Another reason I got into the game was because of the players. It's always more fun to watch a sport if you know some of the players and have a favorite or two. Before, when I'd gone to a baseball game, I didn't know any of the players. I'd never heard their name before. Going to a game with you was exciting because you knew so much about the players and you'd tell me stuff about them. By the time you go to the first dozen games you start to see who the starters are and the pitching rotation. Who will come out in relief. You know the lineup, too. I remember their faces and uniform numbers. I start to recognize their songs they play when they're coming to bat. At that point it's a better time for me because I'm invested. Being a season ticket holder and seeing them play so much I feel like I know the players. I watch them having a good time on the field and joking with the fans. I see Randy Ready coaching third base and making faces at people and talking to someone in the stands between innings. When one of the guys gets cut I get so upset. If someone goes down with an injury I feel so bad for them, like I know them personally."

In November of 2016 the Jacksonville Suns became the Jacksonville Jumbo Shrimp.

The Suns, a team dating back to 1962 in Jacksonville, had been purchased by Ken Babby two years ago with former owner Peter Bragan Jr. staying on in 2015).

I had the privilege to talk with owner Ken Babby about the name change. Was he happy with the community embracing it?

"We are. Everyone's been awesome. Those first few days were rough. I joked we changed the name and then I just hid under my bed for a week. After four or five weeks the lovers started to outweigh the haters. By December we'd shipped merchandise to seventeen countries and all fifty states. By the time Opening Day was here everyone was pretty excited about what was going on. We've had a lot of fun building something the community's quickly fallen in love with. We're very happy about that. And then we're also very grateful this community took a chance on us. We're a bunch of people who aren't from here. We're not part of this community. We feel like there's a chance to build something very special and make a big impact."

I think the most telling thing I learned from Mister Babby was how he introduced himself to me when we first met: as the owner of *your* Jacksonville Jumbo Shrimp.

This was going to be an interesting season of baseball.

Chapter 3: Putting The Roster Together

I love baseball because I love the stats. The roster moves. Watching a player rise through the minor leagues and get to The Show. As a kid collecting baseball cards I was always fascinated more by stats on the backs of cards where players spent time in Pawtucket, Visalia, Reading and Jacksonville. I compared the player's stats to see if they were getting better or worse. Wondered why certain guys never made a bigger impact in the majors, yet had a stellar minor league career.

Collecting baseball cards of the minor league team sets was also fun for me. I could see the players as young, wide-eyed men (which I was at a certain time collecting, thinking it could be me holding the bat in the picture) before they became Major Leaguers and lost the hunger because they were probably actually hungry when the picture was taken. These were the guys struggling day-to-day to make it. Only a small percentage of them actually do.

Once I knew we were going to be seeing a lot of the Jacksonville Jumbo Shrimp games I wanted to get a better idea of the players, and not only the top prospects. I enjoyed watching the fringe guys. Those who'd come off an injury-filled season or signed to the club recently. I liked to see how not only the key superstars on the team would work but how all the pieces fit together.

I knew, realistically, the Miami Marlins organization was going into 2017 positive but realistic. This was a rebuilding year. If they didn't get off to a quick start against the Washington Nationals, who were predicted to run away with the division, and the New York Mets, who would be the only real opponent for the Nats, I saw the Marlins as making some trades and bringing in younger guys.

Guys who would be sent to Jacksonville and force some roster moves.

The New Orleans Baby Cakes are the Triple-A team for the Marlins, one step before the Marlins. Jacksonville Jumbo Shrimp at Double-A. The Jupiter Hammerheads were their Class A-Advanced team. Greensboro Grasshoppers were Class A. Batavia Muckdogs were Class-A Short Season. GCL Marlins are Rookie League and DSL Marlins Foreign Rookie League.

I'll refer to these teams quite a bit, as players get promoted and demoted all season.

Around March I started seeing some names on the transaction wire being outrighted to the Jumbo Shrimp: lefty Dillon Peters, catcher Austin Nola, third baseman Brian Anderson.

In April a flurry of moves to set the roster included shortstop Yefri Perez being reassigned from the New Orleans Baby Cakes as well as righty Tayron Guerrero. Both men were on the Marlins 40 man roster so I was interested in seeing them play and if they could move up to Triple-A and the majors.

Two players moving up from Jacksonville to New Orleans was shortstop Peter Mooney and outfielder Moises Sierra. I wondered if both would have a good enough season to stay in Triple-A.

Overall seventeen of the twenty-five roster spots for Jacksonville were players who'd been here before, including the aforementioned Dillon Peters, who started the year as the Marlins number 5 prospect. He'd pitched four starts for Jacksonville last year after moving up from Jupiter, where he was a 2016 Florida State League All-Star.

The other two starting pitching notables were lefty Matt Tomshaw and righty Chris Mazza, both returning for another season in Jacksonville.

Omar Bencomo and Mike Kickham, both new to the Marlins organization, rounded out the starting rotation for the Jumbo Shrimp.

The bullpen was led by the Marlins number 6 prospect, lefty Jarlin Garcia. The other lefty in the pen was James Buckelew. Righty Tayron Guerrero (the number 16 prospect for the Marlins) was joined by Hunter Adkins and Victor Payano as well as a trio of Tylers: Tyler Kinley, Tyler Higgins, and Tyler Bremer.

Austin Nola would be the primary catcher this year with Cam Maron also behind the plate. It's interesting to note Nola played shortstop for the team in 2014 and 2015.

The infield positions were solid, with the Marlins number 4 prospect Brian Anderson at third and Yefri Perez at second and short. Yefri made his Major

League debut last year in Miami, getting into a dozen games for the Marlins. Infielders Alex Yarbrough, David Vidal, K.C. Serna, and Taylor Ard should also share some playing time.

The outfield is another strong point for the team, with Marlins number 8 prospect Austin Dean in left, a Southern League All-Star in 2016 with more than a few whispers his time in Jacksonville won't be long before he's promoted to Triple-A New Orleans. Jacksonville returning outfielders Jeremias Pineda and Alex Glenn are joined by newcomer to the team John Norwood, who spent 2016 in High-A Jupiter.

What do I think of the team as we get closer to the start of the 2017 season? On paper the team looks solid. While no one would mistake the Marlins minor league system for the Cubs or Red Sox right now, they still have some intriguing players that could catch fire and move up and out of Jacksonville early in the season.

Being a fan of minor league teams means you root for the players but feel sad when they're sent up or down or released. In the perfect world, the twenty-five man roster stays intact all year with no roster moves or injuries.

I know it isn't logical. I'm looking forward to being a season ticket holder and seeing as many games as possible this year, all the while getting to know the Jacksonville Jumbo Shrimp players as much as possible from a fan's perspective.

At some point in the season I'll favor a player or two. Start to really follow their stats and see who's ahead of them in the Marlins depth charts. See who's making a strong case at Single-A and who gets drafted in June to someday take their roster spot in Jacksonville.

It's April and I have no preconceived idea if this team is going to win or lose. No clue which players will make me cheer and which will make me groan.

Don't you just love baseball?

Chapter 4: April 6th - 10th. Opening Series on the road vs. Mississippi Braves

April 6th

Sadly, I didn't get a chance to see any of these games. What a way to start a season as a fan, right? The Jumbo Shrimp took to the road and faced the M-Braves in Pearl, MS. A place I'd be visiting during the summer if all went as planned.

They took the first game of the season and the first as the Jacksonville Jumbo Shrimp with Dillon Peters getting the win. In five innings he allowed a run on three hits. Seven strikeouts, too. He put down the first nine batters he faced. Obviously a good selection for opening day pitcher and someone the organization is high on.

First baseman Taylor Ard started the scoring with a double, knocking in two, in the top of the first. Left fielder Austin Dean had a triple, knocking in two, and second baseman David Vidal added another RBI for a 5-0 lead. Tyler Higgins worked the final two innings to preserve the victory.

April 7th

The Jumbo Shrimp lost to the M-Braves, 2-0. Both teams had some great pitching. Jacksonville starter Matt Tomshaw took the loss, giving up two runs in the first inning. He scattered seven hits with no walks and six strikeouts in five innings of work. Except for the shaky first inning he pitched a great game. Relievers Jarlin Garcia and Victor Payano blanked the M-Braves in the final three frames but the offense couldn't get rolling.

April 8th

The Jumbo Shrimp took the third game of the opening series, 6-1. Starter Omar Bencomo got the win with five scoreless innings in his Marlins debut. He'd started out in the Tampa Bay Rays system as an undrafted free agent in early 2007. He was with them through 2011. In 2013 and 2014 he played in the Venezuelan Winter League before signing with the independent Wichita Wingnuts in 2015. He made it back to the MLB in August of 2015, signing a minor league contract with the Minnesota Twins and staying in their system through 2016. He elected free agency and signed with The Miami Marlins in February 2017. Omar was also selected as a member of Venezuela in the 2017 World Baseball Classic and pitched in three games, once as the starter.

Austin Dean hit the first Jumbo Shrimp homer of the year, a solo shot in the fourth. Brian Anderson had an RBI single in the seventh inning. Dean and Anderson both went 3 for 5 in the game.

April 9th

Another road loss to start the season. Starter Mike Kickham got off to a rocky start, giving up runs in the first two innings. Kickham was a 2010 draft pick of the Giants and made his MLB debut in 2013. When the Giants released him last year he signed with the Kansas City T-Bones of the Independent American Association and made fourteen starts. He was signed by the Marlins a month ago. He settled down after giving up two runs in his debut for the organization, going five innings and allowing four hits with four strikeouts with no decision.

This game went 13 innings with the M-Braves getting the win when Keith Curcio hit a two-run single off of reliever Tyler Bremer. The Jumbo Shrimp had actually taken the lead in the top of the 13th when Austin Dean had an RBI single.

April 10th

Another road loss to start the season. The Jumbo Shrimp fell to 2-3 as the M-Braves took the opening series victory. Chris Mazza took the loss, allowing five runs on seven hits. He walked two and struck out three in five innings. The M-Braves got the win as Mike Soroka, a vaunted prospect in the Braves system, got the win with five scoreless innings in his Double-A debut.

After tomorrow's travel day, a long ride on the bus, the Jumbo Shrimp will make their first homestand of the season.

I'm looking forward to sitting for the first time in our seats.

Section 102. Row J. Seats 1 and 2.

This is going to be a fun summer for me in Jacksonville.

I'm hoping to see some good baseball, get to relax and not worry about writing and bills and deadlines, and also hope my wife catches the baseball bug like I did at an early age and gets even half as excited as I do when I'm watching the game.

Chapter 5: April 12th - 16th. Home Opener vs. Chattanooga Lookouts

April 12th

This is what you wait all winter for. The last out of last season I begin counting the days until the next season, and then to the first pitch of the first game I can attend.

I follow half a dozen blogs about baseball moves. I watch MLB Network all winter, watching the Red Sox free agent signings, roster moves and updating their minor league systems.

Since I wasn't thinking too much about the Marlins I didn't pay close attention to the team and especially not their minor league players.

I went into the opening homestand just hoping to see some quality baseball being played.

The Jacksonville Jumbo Shrimp welcomed 10,477 fans to the ballpark with a win, the biggest Opening Day crowd since the record-setting opening in 2003.

We got to see Dillon Peters get his second win of the season with five and ⅔ innings, only allowing one run on three hits while striking out four. Tyler Higgins looked impressive as well, going 2 ⅔ in relief. Jarlin Garcia worked a perfect ninth, too. If the pitching can keep throwing gems like this they'll easily win the first half.

Taylor Ard's first homer in Double-A was a Grand Slam in the third inning, getting off to a strong start to the season. So far his first taste of Double-A is a good one. It will be interesting to see if he can keep up this torrid pace throughout the 140-game season.

The only bad part was seeing outfielders Austin Dean and Yefri Perez collide in the outfield on a miscue going for a ball. It looks like Dean was injured on the play.

April 13th

I was actually away on a book tour in New Jersey. My wife and I left after last night's game but I followed along on my computer, annoyed I hadn't planned the tour better. I guess making money selling books so I could afford to go to the games was beside the point, right?

I had no idea how great the game was yesterday, and not just the actual win. I missed the open air, the sights, the fans, the food, and the smells… all of it.

When I was sitting in my seat for those three or so hours everything else faded away. I could forget about writing deadlines, personal stuff, bills, the future, the past, and everything else.

Section 102, Row J, seat 1 became my oasis. Those who aren't baseball fans won't understand it. An outsider might look at baseball as a slow, boring sport. I look at it as the perfect pace. I love the strategy. The bunts. The steals. The subtle shifting of a fielder as the ball is thrown. The towering homers and diving catches. Third base coach/manager Randy Ready giving the signs, all the while smiling between pitches and watching the crowd.

Baseball is the one constant in my life, as corny as it sounds.

Of course, during the trip back to New Jersey it wasn't all work. I got to attend a Lakewood Blue Claws game, the Class-A Phillies team. They played the Greensboro Grasshoppers, the Marlins Class-A team. I wish I'd paid more attention to the game but I was too busy eating good food and hanging out with my fellow authors Chuck Buda and Frank Edler and their families, who I never see enough.

As for Jacksonville...

A crowd of 8,249 got to watch for me and see right fielder John Norwood and third baseman Brian Anderson hit back-to-back homeruns.

These two were going to be interesting to watch this year.

April 14th

The Jumbo Shrimp SHUTOUT the Lookouts in front of 10,023 fans. Starter Omar Bencomo went six for his second win of the young season and Victor Payano, Tyler Kinley and Tyler Bremer finished off the game on the pitching side.

It was the first Red Shirt Friday and a fireworks night I missed.

It was also a great night for left-handed pitcher Jarlin Garcia, who got the call up to the Marlins.

I wondered how many more Jumbo Shrimp would follow before the end of the season.

April 15th

The Jumbo Shrimp got shelled, plain and simple. They lost 10-1 in front of 8,821 fans. Starter Mike Kickham looked impressive through the first four innings but gave up two runs on four hits in five innings of work.

Reliever Hunter Adkins gave up three more runs in the sixth. Ryan Beckman made his Jumbo Shrimp debut after being promoted from Short Season-A Batavia Muckdogs but gave up five runs to close out the loss.

Catcher Chris Hoo was activated from the 7-Day DL and left fielder Austin Dean was placed on the 7-Day DL.

It looks like his crash in the outfield the other night will put him out of the lineup for awhile. I got to speak with Austin Dean towards the end of the season, which he missed the bulk of. Despite a huge setback and loss to most of his season, he was upbeat and smiling.

"Injuries happen. I started off good for six games and then the collision in the outfield. That's baseball. It happens. I was devastated when I found out I broke my hand. I was very fortunate I didn't have to have surgery. The rehab process was long and grueling. It was very tough to stay focused down there but I did

what I needed to do. I got my mind back on right. I'm just happy to be back playing," Austin told me.

Was it a thought of a completely lost season?

"Not at first. There were a lot of miscues of when I was going to return. We thought I'd be back in a month. Maybe a couple of weeks. The pain kept lingering. It was in the organization's best interest to keep me down there until the pain was gone completely. I'm happy we went through that decision. They didn't rush me back."

You're down there but are you watching the team and whoever is playing left field for you?

"Absolutely. I kept in touch with everybody. I looked at the stats but really just cared about us winning. How the guys were doing. I kept up with a couple guys like Brian Anderson. He and I have been roommates the past three years, we're both poised on a similar level. There's an expectation. I kept up with him. I texted a few other guys and they all checked up on me and asked when I was coming back. There's a good friendship around here."

April 16th

Chattanooga Lookouts first baseman Jonathan Rodriguez took care of all the scoring with a solo homer in the seventh off of reliever Tayron Guerrero. 3,706 fans came out, making it the highest attendance for a series in the history of the Baseball Grounds, dating back to 2003.

It looks like there are many more people who are fans of the name change than those complaining all offseason.

The team is off to a slow start with a 5-5 record after their first two series.

In a roster move, right hander Ryan Beckman was put on the 7-Day DL. Righty Greg Nappo was assigned from Triple-A New Orleans.

Chapter 6: Dad's A Tigers Fan

I have heroes. In a later chapter I'll fully explain why I'm a Red Sox fan and why Jim Rice was my favorite player. Whether it is sports heroes or musicians and writers or actors, we all have those we look up to. Imagine them in real time as being these amazing people we can learn from. Maybe follow their lead. Listen to what they have to say.

In reality I enjoy reading and watching these people. I don't really follow too many of their examples except an overall reach of trying to be the best I can be.

The one person I always considered a hero from a young age was my father.

Not only did he give me his love of baseball, I always joke in interviews I got my love of reading from my mother and my art of storytelling from my father.

The Rosamilia joke was my father never let facts get in the way of a good story. He could weave a tale about anything and have you believe every word he said was the truth. He'd say it with conviction even when he was telling a tall tale. For him it was in the storytelling. It was the fun of trying to convince you what he said had really happened.

I'm not calling my father a liar. I'm asking you to sit down with him and let him tell you about any interest. Any theme. Any subject. My father is the greatest storyteller you'll ever meet.

More importantly he instilled in me and my brother a sense of worth. The idea you needed to work for your money. You needed to put family first but have fun doing it.

I didn't grow up with a lot of money. My parents struggled. They had me young. My mother was eighteen and my father twenty when I was born. My father served in Vietnam. Saw action. Came home and went to work to support his family.

I didn't know when I was a kid grilled cheese and soup was more about not having extra money for dinner rather than my mother just loved eating it so much.

They struggled as parents with two unruly boys and they built an incredible life for us.

A life with baseball always in-season.

My father taught me discipline. Do the best job I could do. Be the best man I could be.

Did I always do my best? No. I went through a big part of my life going with the flow and not excelling. I wanted to be an author from my first Dean Koontz book at twelve. But I always had my father in my thoughts when I would make a career change or when it came to my kids. I tried to treat them the way I was treated: Awesomely. Plain and simple.

It was a privilege to sit down with my father and ask him specific questions about his love of baseball. Sure, I'd had a thousand conversations about it over the years with him, but this was the first time I could ask questions I've always wanted answers to.

What follows is an interview with my father too long in coming.

How did you become a Tigers fan?

"My father, your peepa, (also Armand Rosamilia - all first males on the Rosamilia side were named Armand. Armando, actually) *was the middleman between Ballantine's brewery in Newark and the Yankees. He was very athletic. They called him Carideo. Frank Carideo was an All-American football player from Notre Dame. They said he played like Frank Carideo so they gave him the nickname. He was also a big baseball and Yankees fan so he was the perfect person. Every Sunday morning Yankees player Elston Howard and his family would come to our house to eat. Whenever there was a doubleheader, which was usually every Sunday. Everyone called him Ellie. His wife and my mother would walk across the street to church. Then the car would come to pick everyone up for the game. Sometimes Yogi Berra, Phil Rizzuto, maybe Joe Collins, would meet at my mother's house before the game, too. We'd go to Yankee Stadium. Get there by eleven o'clock. My mother would make a big pot of meatballs every Sunday. She would tell Ellie if he didn't give her the pot back she wasn't going to make anymore meatballs for him or the team. It would be three hundred meatballs. Between games of the doubleheader the team would eat. Me and your uncle*

Armand and your aunts would spend the early morning helping to make these meatballs. Your meema would put down the white sheet on the table and we'd roll them out. That was my father's gift to the Yankees."

I had no idea.

"While my father went into the dugout to socialize, I'd run to the outfield. My brother loved to see the players and try to hang out with them before the game. I'd be in right field. I must've been six or seven years old. No one else was supposed to be out there. Maybe three or four kids of the Yankees were running around back then. I remember Dale Berra, Yogi's son who became a ballplayer, would hang out with my brother in the dugout. They became friends. I didn't want to be bothered. The old Yankee Stadium right field wall was three feet high. I was out there trying to get balls. During batting practice I'd be out there shagging balls, trying not to get in the way. I'd always get a couple. Put them in my pockets. The Yankees would do their running around the time we got to the stadium. Then they'd go off and the visiting team would do their batting practice and drills. One time I tried to get a ball and missed it. One of the players for the visiting team was running. He stopped and picked up the ball, told me it was a good try and tossed me the ball."

My father is smiling as he's telling me this part of the story.

"That was Al Kaline of the Tigers. My father would call us to the Ballantine's box seats. At the time Ballantine's was sponsoring the Yankees. They had the big three-ring sign in the stadium. We'd

always put the balls into a bucket but I told my father I wanted to keep the one the guy gave me. He asked which guy. I told him it was Kaline. My father called over Ellie and asked him to get Kaline to sign the ball and tell him whose kid I was. He wrote on the ball keep practicing. Someday you'll take my spot. Al Kaline. *From that moment I was an Al Kaline fan and a Tigers fan. Before that I was forced to be a baseball fan."*

You didn't like baseball?

"I loved playing the game. I was good. I hated the Yankees because I hated being trapped in the stadium every Sunday. I would rather be home playing baseball with my friends. My brother loved going to the games because he was a big Yankees fan. My mother would spend the day with some of the ballplayer wives and my sisters. I wasn't allowed to stay home. I had to be with the men watching baseball. Pete Sheehy was the Yankees equipment manager for almost sixty years. My father knew him very well. Whenever my father would ask Pete for a hat or something for me I didn't want it. My brother had a hundred Yankees hats."

I wonder what those hats would be worth now. Not that I'd want them. I guess I also got my hatred of the Yankees from my father, too.

In a later chapter I'll tell you about the baseball trip we made together. Just like old times.

Just like baseball fans.

Chapter 7: April 17 - 21. Away vs. Pensacola Blue Wahoos

April 17

The start of another road trip for the Jumbo Shrimp. So far the Blue Wahoos looked impressive this early in the season with an 8-3 record. Jacksonville was now 5-6 after an opening loss, falling 3-1.

Lefty Dillon Peters suffered his first loss in only 1 ⅔ innings cut short thanks to an injury to his left hand. The only scoring by the Jumbo Shrimp was David Vidal hitting a bases loaded single to score Alex Glenn in the first inning to start the game. After that their bats were silenced.

So far, after a small sample of games, it looks to me like the Jumbo Shrimp need to get some better hitting, especially if the pitching can keep them in games as expected. I'm looking for a couple of players to get in the groove and start hitting with more frequency.

April 18

It's always fun to see a major league player on a rehab assignment. Over the years I got to see quite a few Red Sox players in Trenton or Pawtucket. I remember the day I slipped out of work early and drove from New Jersey to Pawtucket to see Roger Clemens pitch. It was a packed house and exciting.

Marlins shortstop Adeiny Hechavarria was part of the Jumbo Shrimp, even if on a temporary basis while he rehabbed. He went 1-for-4 with a single and run scored.

This game was a battle. The Jumbo Shrimp rallied from four runs down to tie it in the sixth but they left too many men on in the last half of the game and missed quite a few scoring chances to win it, including a bases loaded situation in the top of the eighth. Reliever Tyler Bremer not only took the loss but left the game due to injury.

Batting highlights included a two-run homer from John Norwood.

I had the chance to talk to John during the season. He's a quiet guy who seems focused on making the most of his chances in baseball.

How would you describe your season so far?

"Definitely a learning experience. It's a big jump from High A to Double A. The pitching is better. The speed of the game is faster. The players have more experience and the pitchers know where your holes are and they'll pick you apart if you don't adjust in this league. It's definitely fun playing against better talent. It's one step closer to the Big Leagues."

What kind of adjustments did you have to make coming into the league?

"The ability to keep a steady heart rate. Not try to do too much. Being aware of the game and the situation. You have to be consistent, which is something I'm still working on."

So far his swing has been effortless. I predict a good year for Norwood if he can remain healthy, something a few players are having a hard time with so far in this young season. Pitcher Dillon Peters was placed on the 7-Day DL.

April 19

Another loss to a tough Pensacola team. The Jumbo Shrimp were winning going into the eighth inning thanks to a nice seventh, when Alex Yarbrough had an RBI single to cut the Blue Wahoo lead down to one run, 3-2. In the eighth Jeremias Pineda scored on a throwing error that allowed John Norwood to reach base. Then David Vidal knocked Norwood in followed by another RBI for Taylor Ard.

Then it fell apart for the pitching in the eighth. Tyler Higgins, who had relieved starter Omar Bencomo, was pulled after loading the bases and his team holding a 5-3 lead. Tayron Guerrero relieved him but walked a man and a run in. A bases-clearing single by Pensacola and an error by Norwood led to three runs and a 7-5 lead for the Blue Wahoos, which would hold up.

If they can get their pitching and hitting on the same page they have the talent to string a few wins together this season. So far it isn't happening, though.

Righty pitcher Severino Gonzalez was demoted from Triple-A New Orleans.

April 20

Another loss to Pensacola, who are on fire charging out of the gate this season. Pensacola's Deck McGuire (that's a baseball name right there) got the victory for the Blue Wahoos against the Jumbo Shrimp, who dropped to 5-9.

Starter Mike Kickham took the loss, his second of the season. He allowed seven runs on eight hits.

David Vidal had a solo homerun in one of the only highlights for the Jumbo Shrimp. Alex Glenn hit a triple and knocked in two.

The Blue Wahoos have won four in a row against Jacksonville, who are on a six game losing streak.

Hopefully tomorrow's fifth and final game of this series will garner a rare win.

The Jumbo Shrimp made a few moves with their roster as well, placing Tyler Bremer on the 7-Day DL and adding righty Travis Ballew from the Single-A Jupiter Hammerheads to take his spot.

April 21

Jacksonville fell to 5-10 with another loss to Pensacola. The game was scoreless through seven and starter Chris Mazza looked impressive, scattering three hits with a walk while striking out six.

Tyler Higgins took the loss, his second this season, giving up two runs in the eighth inning and ruining a great pitching performance by Mazza.

I'm hoping a change of scenery will do wonders for the team as they head to Birmingham to face the Barons starting tomorrow.

Catcher Chris Hoo went back on the 7-Day DL with a thumb bruise and center fielder Isaac Galloway was sent down from New Orleans.

Chapter 8: April 22 -26. Away vs. Birmingham Barons

April 22nd

I'm obviously unable to attend these away games but through the magic of radio and the internet I'm able to hear each pitch as if I'm in the stands cheering the Jumbo Shrimp on.

The Director of Broadcasting, Roger Hoover, lets the fans listen in on the action. I have to give a shout out to quite a few people in the Jumbo Shrimp organization but want to start with Roger, who gave me great access to players both home and on the road during the writing of this book. He always took the time to answer a question or email and became a huge asset.

In one of our many conversations I got to talk to him about being the voice of the Jumbo Shrimp and his routine.

What's your daily prep for the broadcast?

"A lot of it is killing two birds with one stone. I'm in charge of our media relations. I maintain the roster. Part of the website. The daily game notes, which takes up most of my time. It's a thirteen page document. Listing out the lineups, all the various

records for the team for the season like what their record is when they're ahead after six innings. Things like that. What color jersey they'll be wearing. That's a big part of it. It's really a team record but it helps me doing my broadcast, too. The coaching staff has it. It's also the player's complete bios like where they went to school and what their stats were. All their current statistics for each guy. I maintain them every day. I also keep a player card on my tablet. I add a lot of articles I find to it. Have their basic info at my fingertips. I'll take a screenshot of the opponent's players so I can easily go through for information. I just try to learn everyday and be as good as I can be. It's a good process of not only taking care of your own team but you get to learn the other team as well. I can also go ahead and get ready for the next series, too."

Is it any different when you're on the road?

"Not really. The game itself is exactly the same. I always approach it the same way. When we're home the only extra I have to do is making sure all the media is printed. Take care of media requests. Other than that it's exactly the same no matter at home or on the road," Roger said with an infectious grin.

Roger's love of the game couldn't help the team as they dropped another game, this time 8-2 to a Barons team that wasn't playing much better than the Jumbo Shrimp so far this season. Both teams now own a 5-11 record.

The pitching fell apart in the eighth inning as they gave up six runs and broke a 2-2 tie. Reliever James Buckelew took the loss, giving up the six runs with only one of them earned.

Starter Severino Gonzalez went 5 ⅔ innings and only allowed two runs on five hits.

Once again it was the late inning relief that foiled plans to win a game.

April 23rd

A win by the Jumbo Shrimp stopped their losing streak at eight. Matt Tomshaw got the win with 5 ⅔ innings, only allowing a run while scattering six hits and four walks. He struck out five.

In the 6-1 victory Austin Nola started the scoring in the second with an RBI single. In the third Brian Anderson hit a two-run single and John Norwood added an RBI double.

Center fielder Yefri Perez, mired in a slump like quite a few of the players so far, hit a two-run triple. This guy has some wheels on him and he stretches an easy double into a triple, flying around the bases.

The difference in this game was the bullpen stepping up and doing a great job. Victor Payano retired all seven hitters he face and struck out five of them. In the ninth Tayron Guerrero loaded up the bases and it looked like another win would be snatched away, but he rallied in epic fashion and struck out three in a row to close the door on Birmingham.

In a roster move right fielder Cal Towey was sent down from New Orleans.

April 24th

Another victory for the Jumbo Shrimp. Omar Bencomo, now 3-0 on the year, had a solid 7 ⅓ innings and only gave up one run on four hits. He struck out ten, the highest of the season for the Jumbo Shrimp. Greg Nappo relieved Omar and got the final two outs of the eighth inning. Tyler Kinley pitched a perfect ninth for his first save.

David Vidal continued his torrid pace on the season, getting a hit to make it ten games in a row for him. So far Vidal looks like a great signing for the Marlins from the independent Atlantic League Somerset Patriots. It was also announced he was named the Southern League Player of the Week.

Cal Towey, recently added to the team, was placed on the 7-Day DL and center fielder Alex Glenn was promoted from Short Season-A Batavia.

April 25th

Another step back with another loss. Jacksonville is 7-11 after losing by a 3-2 score. Mike Kickham, still looking for his first win against three losses, gave up two runs (one earned) in six innings. He struck out nine but it wasn't enough as the Barons won.

In all fairness he was matched against the fifth best prospect in the White Sox system in Michael Kopech, who earned his first Double-A victory.

A highlight for the Jumbo Shrimp was David Vidal hitting in his eleventh straight game.

Righty Ryan Beckman was activated from the disabled list, which meant righty Travis Ballew was sent down to Jupiter in a corresponding move.

My wife has trouble with the many nearly daily roster moves a team has to make. In her perfect baseball world, she'd get to see the same twenty-five players all season long.

I love the chess moves each day with a player being moved and the ripple effect it has on an organization.

April 26th

Jacksonville got off to a 2-0 lead thanks to a walk to Isaac Galloway, second baseman Yefri Perez reaching on a bunt that was thrown away by the pitcher. Again, his quickness comes into play. Brian Anderson smacked a two-run double to left to bring them both home.

The Barons got out of the inning without further damage by pulling off a triple play, their first since 2014. John Norwood walked but DH Alex Glenn lined back to the pitcher, who doubled Anderson off second and on to first to nail Norwood.

Starter Chris Mazza ran out of gas and reliever Tyler Higgins was brought in with a 4-4 tie. He allowed three straight singles and took the loss as the Jumbo Shrimp couldn't rally.

In the sixth inning first baseman Taylor Ard had tied the score with a big home run.

Luckily the team returns home after the bad road trip and I'm hoping they'll rebound and put some wins together. The relief so far has been spotty and the big bats haven't hit with any authority.

But it's still April. Right?

Chapter 9: Mom's A Yankees Fan

I love my mother. Some might even accuse me of being a mama's boy and I gladly accept it. She gave me her love of reading and horror books. She encouraged me to be creative. She never told me not to do something, even if she knew how stupid it was going to be.

I grew up listening to heavy metal music, which she wasn't a fan of but never told me I couldn't. In fact, often enough she wanted to hear what I was listening to and if I understood the message or the meaning behind songs.

For all of that I am forever grateful.

I still hate she's a Yankees fan, though.

As I talked about previously, we're a baseball family. We're also from New Jersey. It means we love to talk loudly (with our hands, too) and argue for the sake of having a good debate. We're passionate about our team and why your team is nothing but a bunch of (insert cheaters/losers/crybabies, etc.) or why my team got ripped off by your team because of (insert frivolous owner/more money/cheating/Babe Ruth, etc.) and any other argument that could be made to keep the heated conversation going.

I can't tell you how many times my mother would remind me how many pennants the Yankees had flying over Yankee Stadium and when the last time the Red Sox had won it all, which until 2004 had been 1918.

By the way, that 1918 chant was horrible. I'm glad I never have to hear that again.

My mother loves to talk about books, TV shows, and the New England Patriots (another team I despise, by the way).

In between talking about all of these things and more, we got around to talking about baseball.

How did you become a Yankees fan?

"I was born a Yankees fan. We used to listen to it on the radio when I was a little kid. We didn't have TV. My brothers would all listen to the games. I loved Mickey Mantle. I've always been a Yankees fan. My sister, your Aunt Kim, was also a Yankees fan. She had a license plate on her car about Lou Piniella. Then she met her future husband, Ron, and was suddenly a Mets fan like him. She became a traitor. I've never forgiven her for it, either. She turned her back on the Yankees for the Mets?"

Like my dad, my mother also grew up in a baseball family.

Then she met my father.

"When we were dating we'd go to see the Yankees. All the home games, which I loved and he hated."

I can only imagine the epic fights my parents would have about baseball in the 60's.

I have to give it to her, though. Even when the Yankees were going through the lean years and losing more than winning, she stuck by them.

Even with Billy Martin in and out of the manager's seat she cheered for her Bronx Bombers.

"My first real love of the Yankees was Thurman Munson. I loved him so much. I still remember when he died. I was cooking dinner and you and your brother were watching TV and it came on. You both came into the kitchen and told me. I didn't believe you. I shut the stove and went to watch the TV. They were talking about it and your father pulled into the driveway from work. You and your brother ran outside to let him know. I was crying. Devastated. It was awful. I loved him so much. Then your uncle Bobby would make a paper airplane every year, set it on fire and throw it at me on the anniversary. He was a Yankees fan, too, but he knew how much I loved Thurman."

Catcher Thurman Munson played his entire eleven year career with the Yankees. He's the only Yankee player to win both Rookie of The Year and Most Valuable Player. The first team captain since Lou Gehrig, he led them to three consecutive World Series appearances in 1976, 1977 and 1978.

He was a player I gave begrudging respect to, even as a kid. I knew he was an amazing ballplayer.

Thurman died on August 2nd 1979 at the age of 32 while practicing landing his plane.

As we're talking I can see she's still bothered by his death all these years later.

"After Thurman it was Don Mattingly. Later I was a Jeter fan. Never liked A-Rod. I didn't care for him. He was never a real Yankee player to me."

Of course, once George Steinbrenner figured out which players to overpay and buy himself a few World Series rings… sorry, I won't rant about her team again.

I'll save it for the next time I call her on the phone or go down to my parent's house to argue in person.

Chapter 10: April 27 - May 1. Home vs. Mobile BayBears

April 27th

5,019 of us were at the Baseball Grounds to see the Jumbo Shrimp against the visiting Mobile BayBears. We also saw a loss.

It was tied into the eighth inning until Mobile exploded for five runs. Starter Severino Gonzalez went six and gave up two earned runs and an unearned run. Victor Payano pitched a great seventh but struggled in the eighth, walking the first two batters he faced. He was relieved by Tyler Kinley, who walked a BayBear to load the bases. First baseman Taylor Ard botched a ground ball and Mobile scored the go-ahead run. Add a two-run double and a two-run single and Mobile had the lead and the game.

Notable for the Jumbo Shrimp: Brian Anderson hit a solo homer in the first inning and right fielder John Norwood had an amazing throw with the bases loaded to nail a runner at the plate and end the inning still tied at 3.

April 28th

Friday night fireworks weren't just in the sky. It was on the field, as the Jumbo Shrimp won 4-0 in front of 7,341 fans.

Starter Matt Tomshaw went seven innings without giving up a run. Second baseman David Vidal hit a two-run homer, his second of the season, in the sixth inning.

Ryan Beckman relieved Tomshaw and pitched a scoreless eighth and ninth to earn his first save on the season.

The Jumbo Shrimp need more games like this, where the pitching is above average and the team is getting some runs and jumping to early leads.

April 29th

Right fielder John Norwood and first baseman Taylor Ard both connected for their third home runs of the season in the third. Omar Bencomo is now 4-0 on the season, going five innings and only giving up one earned run on six hits. Tyler Kinley picked up his second save of the season. David Vidal continued his torrid hitting streak, now at fourteen games.

Jacksonville won 4-2 in front of 7,912 on a nice Saturday night. After the game the Boy Scouts had a sleepover in the outfield.

Another perfect game as far as I was concerned. The pitching and hitting were on tonight. If they can keep this up they'll have a chance to turn around the first half of the season and make the playoffs.

The Jumbo Shrimp placed pitcher Tayron Guerrero on the 7-Day DL and added righty Joe Gunkel to the roster in a corresponding move.

Joe Gunkel was a recent signing after the Los Angeles Dodgers released him. He'd started his career in the Red Sox organization, so of course I had to talk to him. During the season we sat down for a chat.

How is pitching for the Marlins different?

"The people are different. There are little things in each organization that differ. At the end of the day it's nine guys on the field trying to get better and win ballgames."

How do you like pitching in the Southern League?

"I haven't had much success in this league as I've had in others. The travel is tough. It's hot everywhere we go. There are some good pitcher's ballparks and some hitter's ballparks."

So for you, who were some of your baseball idols?

"I was always a Phillies fan. My dad was born in the Philadelphia area. Early 2000's is when I really started getting into it. I was eight or nine years old. I was a big Jim Thome fan. He was with the Phillies in '02/'03. I played first base and outfield growing up. Jim Thome and Aaron Rowand, when he was with the Phillies, were my favorites. I got to high school and I was more into Chase Utley, Jimmy Rollins and Ryan Howard and that era. The 2008 championship team. That was fun to see."

When did you switch to pitcher?

"High school. I pitched a little bit when I was younger but I was never any good. I was a late bloomer. In high school I really wanted to play outfield. I didn't want to do anything else but they convinced me to pitch. I said I'd give it a shot. After my sophomore year I started to get a lot better. My velocity started to come along. Junior year I started to talk to colleges. That's when I went into full pitcher mode. I wanted to still play the field in college, which I kinda did my freshman year but then I went full-time pitching. I realized myself I was a better pitcher than fielder or hitter. I just stuck to pitching. All my time and energy into it. See where it takes me."

Feelings when you were first drafted.

"It was cool. No one I ever knew had gotten drafted. I didn't really know what to expect. I was down in North Carolina in the Coastal Plains League in Moorehead City when I found out. Another guy on our team got drafted so we had that cool moment where we got to talk about it. I was home for a few days before I flew down to Florida and the Gulf Coast League. It happens so fast you don't get time to process it. Everyone's congratulating you like your family but then you're off. It took a few weeks to acclimate but once I got up to Short Season in Lowell it was pretty cool."

Who did you play with in Lowell?

"Kyle Martin. He was up for a little bit this year. I played with Sam Travis when I was in Salem in 2015. I missed playing with Benintendi."

Of course I had to ask him some Red Sox questions. Right?

April 30th

This is how you win a ballgame. John Norwood hit his fourth home run of the season in dramatic fashion, taking the first pitch in the bottom of the eleventh inning and putting it out of the park. 6,260 got to see great Sunday baseball. Kids played catch in the outfield before the game. I didn't see any still-sleeping Boy Scouts, either.

The game was scoreless until the sixth. Starter Joe Gunkel, making his debut for the team and the Marlins organization, coasted through the fourth before James Buckelew came in for relief. Lefty Greg Nappo and righty Ryan Beckman each worked two scoreless innings. The pitching kept them in the game until Norwood's dramatic homer.

May 1st

Noon game. Daytime baseball. Gotta love it. Shelly couldn't make it. Something about having to work to pay the bills while I took the afternoon off to watch baseball.

I don't remember. I wasn't really listening. Too busy wondering how I was going to get my Diet Coke and two jumbo beef hot dogs by myself.

Before I recap the game, which was great, I need to explain a few rituals I have for a baseball game. I never, ever leave a game before the last out. I don't care what the score is. As long as they're playing I'm in my seat watching.

Once I arrive at the ballpark and sit down I am down for the next few hours. I don't wander around the stadium. I don't take a break to get food and drink. I certainly don't stand up to do The Wave. The Seventh Inning Stretch is baseball so I'll get up and actually stretch.

My wife has figured out this system. Maybe I told her. While she enjoys the games she can't sit for three straight hours without moving.

We'll start the game with a Diet Coke in a Jumbo Shrimp souvenir cup. By the end of the season we had over sixty of them in huge stacks in my Red Sox Room.

Yes, I said Red Sox Room. More on that in a later chapter.

At about the third inning she'll get up when the visitors are batting and stand in line to get us food. A couple of hot dogs, maybe a Jumbo Shrimp helmet filled with nachos. We have over a dozen of them by the season's end, too.

If she's feeling particularly wild she might get us ice cream (also in a helmet but a smaller one) or a pretzel.

All so I don't have to miss a pitch of the game.

She's a keeper.

Anyway… noon game. It's hot. I'm still in my seat. Over 2,000 fans in the stands.

If I was looking for a pitching duel I was sadly disappointed.

Tied 11-11 going into the ninth inning, the Jumbo Shrimp won it in dramatic fashion. Alex Yarbrough started the inning striking out. Isaac Galloway popped up. Two out.

Yefri Perez draws a walk. Brian Anderson doubles to center field and Yefri scores for the win. It was a nail-biter.

Jacksonville had a few homers in this game. Taylor Ard hit his fourth, Alex Glenn got his first, John Norwood (who is on fire at this point) got his fifth and Brian Anderson got his third.

I went home (supposedly to work and write but really to take a quick nap before my wife got home) happy and loving this team. If only they could put it together like this on a consistent basis.

The Jumbo Shrimp placed righty Hunter Adkins on the 7-Day DL and called up lefty Raudel Lazo from Batavia. They also released pitcher Tyler Bremer. You never want to see a guy cut but he seemed to be struggling and someone decided it was time.

May 2nd

The team had the day off. Travel day to Tennessee. I actually had to write books and couldn't attend or listen to a game.

Sometimes life is hard.

Maybe not for center fielder Isaac Galloway, who was promoted to Triple-A New Orleans today.

Chapter 11: May 3 - 7. Away vs. Tennessee Smokies

May 3rd

In the opener to the series the Jumbo Shrimp (now 11-16) lost to the Smokies (16-10) by a 2-1 score. Severino Gonzalez got his first loss of the year, giving up two runs on four hits. He walked one and struck out three in six innings.

James Buckelew relieved him, pitching two scoreless innings, but it was too late.

Jacksonville got eight hits but only one run, a two out RBI single by Austin Nola in the top of the first.

The loss ended the Jumbo Shrimp four-game winning streak.

Not a good way to start a series against one of the tougher teams in the league.

Pitcher Greg Nappo was promoted to Triple-A New Orleans and catcher Chris Hoo was activated from the disabled list.

May 4th

This was more like it. I guess if the Jumbo Shrimp can't simply blow out their opponents, winning in dramatic fashion is the way to do it.

Trailing 2-1 going into the ninth, the Jumbo Shrimp got singles from David Vidal, Taylor Ard, Cam Maron and KC Serna and put them ahead 3-2. Alex Glenn knocked in another run with a groundout and Brian Anderson hit a two-run double to make it 6-2.

Even though reliever Ryan Beckman blew a save opportunity he got the win. Victor Payano got the final out to get his first save of the season.

It was the first victory in fifteen games the Jumbo Shrimp had been trailing after eight innings.

Lefty Kyle Lobstein was added to the Jumbo Shrimp roster from extended spring training.

May 5th

Postponed due to rain. I couldn't listen to a game tonight, which throws my routine off. I'm definitely a creature of habit and when my schedule is changed, especially last-minute, it messes with me.

I was really enjoying the play-by-play of Roger Hoover (Director of Broadcasting) and Marco LaNave (Media & Public Relations Manager) on these away games. I should also mention again how generous both men were with their time and their patience with all of my questions.

During the season I had the pleasure of interviewing both men.

I asked Roger how he got started in broadcasting.

"When I was in college I did a lot of work in sports broadcasting. I was a reporter at the University of Tennessee. That led to a little play-by-play with the Tennessee volleyball team and soccer. My first real stepping into baseball play-by-play was 2008 with the Kingsport Mets. Kingsport Tennessee is my hometown. I did that for one summer. From there I got a job with the Tennessee Smokies, Double-A club for the Cubs. I was in the Southern League as a broadcast assistant there. I did two or three innings a night. Home games and back in the studio when the team was on the road. That was 2009 and 2010. Being around the Southern League I was able to make some contacts. I got hired by Jacksonville in 2011. I actually left after a year and went back to Tennessee and took a broadcasting job with the University of Tennessee calling a lot of their baseball games. Jacksonville made me another offer so I came back and I've been here ever since. It's my tenth year in baseball and ninth in the Southern League."

This is the second season Roger and Marco are working together in the radio booth.

What did Marco do before this?

"I was in Davenport Iowa with the Quad Cities River Bandits, a Single-A team in the Midwest League. It was an affiliate of the St. Louis Cardinals for one season I was there and then for three seasons they were a Houston Astros affiliate. I was the Director of Media Relations and Broadcasting. I was the voice and did play-by-play for all four seasons."

Is broadcasting something Roger has always wanted to do?

"Yes. I grew up a big Chicago Cubs fan in Tennessee. It was back when WGN was carrying every Cubs game. I was a big fan of Harry Caray and Steve Stone. They were my babysitters. My dad grew up a big Cubs fan in the fifties. He passed on his love of the team to me. I spent time every summer from about the age of five making a trip to Chicago to see the Cubs for a weekend or a week. We'd meet them a lot when they were on the road in Cincinnati or Atlanta. I always knew I wanted to work in sports somehow. I realized broadcasting was the perfect mix of the things I liked to do. It's performing when I'm on the air. I get the performer's rush. My mom worked in music, my dad in theater. It drew me to it. I've always been fascinated by broadcasting. I was always more interested in the broadcaster's personalities than the game. It started before I went to college. I was a public address announcer in high school. Volleyball. Baseball. Softball."

Marco, how is it different now being part of the Jumbo Shrimp, especially with the name change?

"This season has been unlike any other I've worked in baseball. It was very exciting for me when I found out we were doing it. This being my sixth season in minor league baseball, it's the first time I've ever been a part of a refresh and rebrand. It was a little nerve-wracking. I felt good about the people we had in place here. The leadership. Ken Babby, the owner. Harold Craw, the GM. I'd worked with Harold in Davenport. That's how I knew him previously. That's how I got connected here."

I'm seeing a lot of those stories so far. Who you know in minor league baseball.

Marco agrees.

"You can talk to anyone in this business and see the connections. Either a mutual connection or a connection through a connection. You find out you're related to them somehow. It speaks to the tight-knit world of baseball. Coming to Jacksonville I could sense there was a lot of tradition here. Throughout the twentieth century. Going back before it was the Jacksonville Suns. I think it is part of what made me nervous. I've been a baseball fan a long time. My hometown team in St. Cloud Minnesota, the one I grew up following, was a summer college league team, they were called the St. Cloud River Bats. They were the team I followed and loved as a kid. Towards the end of college they had an ownership change and changed the name to the St. Cloud Rox. It was the name of a minor league team that had played there back in the forties until the seventies. That connected to St. Cloud heritage but at the same time I grew up with the River Bats. It took a little bit of adjusting to get used to the change for me. There's a piece of me that misses the River Bats. The nostalgia of it for me. It's not exactly what the people in Jacksonville went through but it's a small part of that, I think."

Roger, there's a learning curve to the advancements in technology. How has that affected your career?

"A lot of the things we do every day haven't changed a ton. Since I first got into baseball in 2008, we're still using phone lines back to our radio station. That will eventually go away. A lot of the

phone issues and tech stuff would keep me up at night. It's also just easier still using that technology to connect these days, too. The process overall is a lot easier now than when I started. I'm someone who's always tried to stay on the cutting edge."

Was it hard in the beginning to not still call them the Suns, Marco?

"I think it only took me a couple of days on the phone and then maybe there was once or twice in the offseason I slipped. For me it had only been a year earlier I would slip and start to say Quad Cities River Bandits. The transition definitely wasn't as hard for me as it was for other people. Doing the repetitions was helpful and then earlier in the broadcast year there were a couple of times I almost slipped but was seriously impressed because the first series was on the road and Roger was there calling the games. I was back in the studio in Jacksonville helping the producers. I couldn't believe how well Roger did calling them Jumbo Shrimp the entire time. He'd called five seasons of Jacksonville Suns. It was incredible. A credit to him."

How is it working with Roger?

"It's great. This is our second year together. We're a step ahead of where we were a year ago. Going into this season both of us were really excited because we had a year under our belt together. We knew how each other operated. With the training of other producers I could anticipate what he was going to do and explain to them how it would all fit together. I think both of us knew the vision of the Jumbo Shrimp and we were both excited about this year. He's a great professional. When I was coming

here that was a big point I wanted to know more about. Looking at the opportunity here was, if I was going to be sharing a broadcast booth, could I work with this person? Because I'd been in his chair for the last four years. What would it be like working with someone on a different level? But Roger welcomed me in and we got to know each other really well. We're less than a year apart in age. We can relate on a professional level, a personal level, and know where each other is at. It has been a lot of fun to work with Roger. He loves the game of baseball. He loves Jacksonville. He wants our broadcasts to be fun but still top of the line professional. It's also something I want to have. I think he's made me a better broadcaster and a better person in the job I do."

I asked Roger: with so many prospects in this league, are you focusing on them before and during the game?

"Yes. Something I've always done on my scorecard is highlight the top prospects. I use Baseball America Top 30 Handbook *for each organization. I mark what number prospect they are for the other team. During some broadcasts it also allows me to get into some fun stuff like random things about what the team is doing or other facts. But when the prospects are pitching or are batting I try to focus on telling their story. Something I always have to keep in mind is when we're at home MiLB.com always takes our home feed and put into clips. So if a prospect for the other team hits a homerun, that clip will make its way around the internet. It will be there forever. I always try to give that a pretty good call. Even if it's against*

Jacksonville I try to give it a professional call just because I know it's me also out there."

Marco, what other things are you doing besides sitting in the booth with Roger?

"I do ticketing group sales. My cubicle is actually in the group sales office. A lot of my offseason is actually spent on the phone, meeting people, selling season tickets, selling groups and then working on the other public relations aspects. We've got several hands on the social media accounts. I'm on a small piece of them so I really can't take credit for the wit we have on social media. That's our assistant GM, Noel. Things like the website. Getting ready for the season. The press releases. With the rebrand it was a bigger role. Planning out the press conference. Making sure everything was ready to go without incident. I think that's one of my strengths that I bring here. Making sure we have all of our details covered. Sometimes I'll just ask questions to make sure we've got all our bases covered. It's been fun to be part of the team here."

Roger, what kind of relationship do you have with the players, and does it differ between the prospects and the marginal guys?

"Not really. The only way it differs is I might have a few more media requests. I line them up and might have a few more for a prospect than another player. I try to treat every guy the exact same way. I'm not too involved with what they're doing. I'm very friendly with the players and we have a great relationship but I'll never try to be buddies with them. Stay at arm's length as much as I can and stay professional. I'm still on the other side. We're

naturally closer because I travel with the team. The wall in minor league baseball is broken down more than in the majors. There still needs to be some separation between the players and everyone else. Most of my friendships with players have happened after they've left Jacksonville. Then we'll stay in touch of Facebook or Twitter. Then when I go to Miami for ballgames or spring training its fun reconnecting with them. I try to also be respectful of their personal space. These guys are busy enough. The last thing they need is me being their cheerleader or a hanger-on."

Marco, had you done the on-field after-game interviews before?

"In Quad Cities I had done pregame on-field interviews similar to what I do in-game during the fifth inning here. Doing a post-game interview live was a new thing for me. Doing it on camera in front of the crowd. I had to adjust to it. I've been in front of a crowd doing interviews before so it wasn't all that different. It's a fun part of my role, having all those broadcast elements I get to be involved with."

Are you cognizant at all times someone like Austin Dean is coming out with water or something to throw at who you're interviewing?

Marco laughed. *"He's done it every game so I'm prepared for it. I'm a little worried, though, because they've started taking aim at me. The big thing when I worked with Roger last year, a couple of times he took a Gatorade bath because Austin hit a walk-off homer or something, and Roger would say make sure you describe what is going on both on the video board and in the stands because people on the radio need to know what's going on. You can't just go silent on the microphone. So when guys get doused you'll hear me say 'oh, here comes a water bottle from Austin Dean' so people on the radio can hear what's going on. I've had colleagues remark how I kept it together. You took that water like a champ. I have to be ready to adjust on the fly."*

Are some guys reticent about doing media, Roger?

"Sometimes. If guys have gone to college they're usually much better prepared for the media. In every school you've got local TV stations, studio newspaper and radio, as well as websites devoted to covering the schools and teams. They get used to it. After being under such scrutiny in college most players find there is less media attention now. Dillon Peters, for instance, was at University of Texas. They have their own network and show every single game. They have daily interviews and cameras in the clubhouse. Here the demand is a little less. We get it every now and then. Not close to what it is for most major college programs. For other guys who were in high school and then drafted into the organization they're not used to it as much. Overall everyone does a pretty good job of it. It also seems to me that the guys who are in demand do a better job than anyone else. For them it's just a conversation. They want to get it done. They enjoy it but it's not a major thing for them."

I asked Marco the final question: Was the name change hard to explain? Some people don't get this is the natural progression of the minor leagues with the name changes and having fun with it.

"Yeah. When we could point to other teams in the league like the Montgomery Biscuits, Pensacola Blue Wahoos, and Biloxi Shuckers and say we actually really fit in with this. It was a great point for us to be able to make. I think we handled it about as well as we could have. It definitely engaged the people of Jacksonville and the fan base. You're never expecting everyone to get onboard right away. That would be unreasonable. What the team in Akron went through three years earlier, the change from the Aeros to the Rubber Ducks, was our template for how this was going to unfold. It was such a great help for me to be able to talk to my counterpart up in Akron who had just been through this. He could tell me what to prepare for and how it went down for him. I'm someone who's intense and about the details. To have that kind of reassurance was pretty remarkable and really helped me do a much better job in that role."

May 6th

A nasty day to play baseball. The second game of the doubleheader was abandoned due to the cold and a lengthy rain delay so they played one seven inning game that the Jumbo Shrimp lost 7-4.

Starter Joe Gunkel took the loss in less than ideal pitching conditions, allowing four runs in four innings. Raudel Lazo was ineffective in relief, walking four batters including one with the bases loaded. Kyle Lobstein came in to finish off the last 1 ⅓ inning. He had a wild pitch that brought in another run. Overall not a good pitching performance from the team.

It looks like tomorrow the teams will squeeze in a doubleheader, weather permitting.

Pitcher Greg Nappo was back in uniform from New Orleans and pitcher Victor Payano was moved up to the Triple-A club.

May 7th

The Jumbo Shrimp and the Smokies split a doubleheader, giving Tennessee three out of the five games. This will be the only away series for the Shrimp to play the Smokies.

In the first game the Jumbo Shrimp lost 9-2. Omar Bencomo is now 4-1 after allowing nine runs on eight hits in 4 ⅓ innings.

The Jumbo Shrimp fared better in game two, winning 3-0. Starting pitcher Chris Mazza went four scoreless innings but Hunter Adkins got the win, his first of the year, with two innings of relief. Ryan Beckman earned his second save to close out the game.

Brian Anderson hit another first inning home run and drove in all three runs with the blast. He's really on a tear lately.

Righty Hunter Adkins was activated from the disabled list and lefty Greg Nappo was promoted to New Orleans.

Chapter 12: I'm A Red Sox Fan

Jim Rice. Number 14. 1975.

My earliest Red Sox memories are of Rice and his huge arms wearing his red baseball cap and hitting home runs. I can picture his batting stance and it still means power to me. The guy was focused. He was intimidating. He was my first real focus when we went to see the games at Fenway Park.

I think if I counted all the games I've ever gone to, the bulk of my Major League baseball games would be in Fenway Park. Even though we lived much closer to Yankee Stadium and Shea Stadium and the Mets or Veteran's Stadium and the Phillies, as a kid we used to go north and inevitably get to Fenway Park.

"In the beginning the vacations to New England were based around what you and your brother were learning in school. You'd learn about Plymouth Rock so we'd take you during the summer to see it. One year we were vacationing in Massachusetts and decided to go to a Red Sox game. Rod Carew was hitting .400 at the time. It was towards the end of the season and I was a baseball fanatic. If we had to take you and your brother on vacation for stuff I was going to get to see a baseball game," my dad said.

I'm sure we didn't go on vacation to New England every summer when I was a kid, but it felt like it. For me it was something to look forward to. While I've always been a history nerd, even as a kid, the baseball games were what I most looked forward to.

Obviously I don't remember every game we went to. I never saved anything from them to let me know the dates. I do, however, have a romantic image in my head about seeing Jim Rice for the first time in his rookie year and he hit two home runs that day.

That might or might not have happened. In my mind… it did.

I do know I was in awe of him as a player, more than any other on the field.

I started asking for Red Sox hats and jerseys, which wasn't an easy thing to get in the 1970's growing up in New Jersey. There was no internet shopping, no stores that carried every conceivable team. It was very local. You had two choices: Yankees or Mets. If you traveled to South Jersey you might see some Phillies merchandise.

That was it.

"One of the big things going to a game at Fenway was going to the big store across the street. We all bought jackets and hats. It was a June game and it was cold. There were no Tigers jackets but mom got a Yankees jacket. You got a Red Sox hat and jacket. We were underneath the right field overhang and it was freezing. We stuck it out," mom said.

I'm still annoyed they sold Yankees items so close to Fenway Park.

My dad used to subscribe to *The Sporting News* and every week a new issue of the oversized newspaper would arrive. If I heard the mailman I'd rush to the door to get it, ignoring boring stuff like bills and catalogs.

By the time my dad came home from work I'd have read through most of it, especially during baseball season. I can remember going through box scores and league leader charts to see where Jim Rice and the other Red Sox players were on the lists.

I'd pay attention to the baseball schedule to see when the Red Sox were playing the Yankees, which was the only time I'd be able to see them on television. It wasn't like it is today with so many games against a division opponent. It was a balanced schedule and no interleague, so seeing them against the Mets was unheard of… except the World Series.

Like in 1986.

I proudly wore my Red Sox blue satin jacket and my Red Sox cap to school every day. I was in tenth grade. All of my friends were Yankees fans. A couple of them were Mets fans.

Once October rolled around and the World Series started suddenly more of them were Mets fans than ever before.

My buddy Dan was over during Game Six. I can still remember the feeling of witnessing something special because the Red Sox were going to win their first World Series since 1918.

This was it.

When the ball went through Buckner's legs I stood up. I remember I couldn't look at my family or my friend. I went upstairs and collapsed on my bed. I never even said goodnight.

When they lost the World Series none of my friends, even the Mets fans or those who'd suddenly become Mets fans, had the heart to bust my chops. I guess they could see the pain etched on my face.

I remember a string of heartbreaking games in subsequent years, all falling short of the World Series and always managing to miss out after battling to get to the postseason.

Aaron Boone's home run off of Wakefield in 2003 was another game I dragged myself to bed after without a word. My parents were there, too. I think they were a *mush* for me.

2004… hey, I'm a diehard Red Sox fan. I thought something horrific would happen. Any true Red Sox fan who says they knew the team would come back to beat the Yankees in dramatic fashion is delusional or not telling the truth.

Dave Roberts stealing the base. I could see the tide turning and I really wanted to believe.

But I'd been here before. Many times.

Winning the last four games in a row? Unheard of. It had never happened in baseball. Yet… they did it.

I remember watching the seventh game alone. My kids were asleep.

The Red Sox won. They were going to the World Series. I got emotional. I admit it.

I knew in my heart they'd gotten past the dreaded Yankees.

No way could they lose to the Cardinals.

I know as a Red Sox fan you can never, ever take anything for granted. There are no easy victories and nothing is ever over 'til it's over.

But it was over.

When they swept the Cardinals in four without ever trailing through the series I knew it was finally destiny. They'd finally done it.

How many generations of Red Sox fans had been waiting for this victory?

I wondered how many men and women had gone to their grave without seeing the Red Sox win a World Series.

Of course, the comeback from the Yankees fans was 'see you in 86 more years' until 2007 when they won it again, this time sweeping the Colorado Rockies.

That shut them up. In 2013 they against defeated the Cardinals in the World Series, although at least St. Louis won two games in it.

Is the magic gone? Are the Red Sox no longer the cursed team who can't win the big game? Yes and no.

The mystique of never winning against their foes has been vanquished. They are a perennial powerhouse in the American League. They stand toe to toe with the Yankees not only in wins and losses but in payroll and securing key free agents.

As long as the Yankees keep grinding it out against my Red Sox there will be something to play for and something for me to bite my nails and watch.

Maybe the next time the Red Sox are in the World Series I can watch it in my Red Sox Room.

Yes, I have a room in my house (formerly my son Jamie's room but he's 22 and on his own) filled with all of my Red Sox memorabilia and baseball cards.

When he moved out my wife wanted to convert his room into another guest room. We have three extra bedrooms in our house. Well, technically extra.

My daughter Katelynn's room is also my wife's Wonder Woman Room. Old school Wonder Woman. Lots of Linda Carter Wonder Woman and really old stuff like comic books and records.

My wife also has a Disney Room, which doubles as the bedroom for our godson James when he's around. Yes, she has Minions in there but Disney and Minions Room is too long to say all the time.

Now I have my own room. I mean, I also have an office filled with all of my books, zombie stuff, comic book stuff, writing stuff and piles of stuff I should really go through.

My Red Sox Room is awesome. Even the bedding is Red Sox. The Pillows.

The best part is when my writing buddies from New Jersey come to visit, like Chuck Buda. He is a Yankees fan and gets to sleep in my Red Sox Room while he's visiting.

I'm going to guess my mother, if she ever stayed at our house again, wouldn't sleep in that room.

Chapter 13: May 8 - 12. Home vs. Biloxi Shuckers

May 8

Being such a Red Sox fan, I always keep tabs on players in their system or ones who've been traded but are making an impact in a new organization. Case in point: I'm a big fan of Anthony Rizzo, who came up in the Red Sox minor leagues.

Mauricio Dubon is another one I still follow. He was traded to the Milwaukee Brewers as part of the package to get Tyler Thornburg. What he lacks in power he makes up for with speed. I could see Dubon manning second base for the Brewers for years to come. He has that much upside. To me, anyway.

Dubon started the scoring for the Shuckers with an infield single due to his speed. He then promptly stole second and was knocked in.

The Shuckers had fifteen hits and won 7-5 in front of 2,890 humans and a lot of dogs. Not hot dogs. Actual dogs as pet owners were allowed to bring their furry friends to see the game for Bark In The Park.

Severino Gonzalez (0-2) took the loss. The Jumbo Shrimp scattered nine hits but the pitching kept letting the Shuckers back in the game.

May 9th

Jacksonville lost 6-4 to Biloxi in front of 2,606 fans on a beautiful clear night. The Jumbo Shrimp bats came alive as Austin Nola hit his first homer and John Norwood hit his fifth of the season, leading the team. Alex Yarbrough went 2-4 and is hitting .305 on the season so far.

I had the pleasure of talking to Alex during the season.

Was there a big difference coming into the Marlins organization?

"For the most part it's just baseball. I was with the Angels for five years. You get used to those people and how everything works. Especially in spring training, where you know where everything is. Who to go to for certain things. After a week or so it really is just baseball. The Marlins run spring training pretty much the same way the Angels did. It's the first time for me playing in this league, which is a different experience. Especially the five-game series. It's something I have to get used to. The travel you have. From Jacksonville our shortest trip is five hours to Pensacola. Most are at least seven or eight. Obviously I've had those kinds of trips before playing in the Texas League but getting in at four a.m. or later happens a lot in this league and then you have to turn around and play that day. It's tough but I've enjoyed it all."

I'll have more on my conversation with Alex Yarbrough later on, too.

In roster moves, pitcher Tyler Kinley was sent down to Jupiter and shortstop KC Serna was promoted to New Orleans. Pitcher Esmerling De La Rosa was promoted from Jupiter to the Jumbo Shrimp.

May 10th

The Biloxi Shuckers defeated the Jumbo Shrimp 3-1 even though it was National Shrimp Day. 3,934 fans turned out on a warm and sunny afternoon of baseball. Once again my wife had to work so I went solo and got my food and drink before I sat in my seat and baked.

Mike Kickham went six scoreless innings and scattered seven hits but the bullpen took the loss as Esmerling De La Rosa started his relief appearance by hitting a batter. In two innings he gave up three hits and three runs and took the loss.

The offense had six hits and looked sluggish. Alex Yarbrough had a single and is on a ten-game hitting streak.

Jacksonville now sits at 13-20 on the season.

Right fielder Cal Towey was activated from the disabled list.

May 11th

Starter Chris Mazza looked solid until the fifth inning when he gave up a solo homer. He allowed three hits and had three strikeouts. Reliever Kyle

Lobstein worked two innings and gave up a run when Mauricio Dubon singled, went to second base on a groundout and promptly stole third, scoring on Austin Nola's passed ball.

Jacksonville made it a game in the ninth with an RBI double by David Vidal and Yefri Perez had an RBI groundout but then they were shut down by Biloxi pitcher Matt Ramsey, who played for the Suns in 2016.

Pitcher Greg Nappo was back from New Orleans again. I imagine he's stopped unpacking his suitcase at this point, bouncing up and down between Double-A and Triple-A so much.

May 12th

David Vidal tried to single-handedly win the fifth and final game of this set with four hits but the Jumbo Shrimp fell short and were swept. 6,904 watched the heartbreaking 4-3 loss but then we were treated to a dazzling fireworks display.

Starter Omar Bencomo went six innings and gave up three runs before Hunter Adkins came in and pitched a scoreless inning.

In the seventh shortstop Alex Yarbrough tried to score from second on a hit by John Norwood but was thrown out at the plate.

Jumbo Shrimp manager Randy Ready disagreed, letting the home plate umpire know the call was wrong. He was ejected and we cheered for Randy as he left the field.

It was tied going into the ninth but Greg Nappo gave up a leadoff single to Mauricio Dubon. This guy is trouble on the base paths for the Jumbo Shrimp. An error moved him to third and a two-out single scored him.

Third baseman Rehiner Cordova was assigned to the Jumbo Shrimp and pitcher Joe Gunkel was designated for assignment and cleared waivers, outrighted to the Jumbo Shrimp. Yefri Perez was also designated for assignment.

Designating a player for assignment (DFA) means he's immediately removed from the parent club's 40-man roster. There are a few options from this point: within 10 days he is returned to the 40-man roster, he's traded or released, he's placed on waivers within the first 7 days, or he's outrighted to the minor leagues.

Teams will use this option when they need to add a player to their 40-man roster and a fringe player they feel won't be claimed by another team when placed on waivers can go through this system. A player might be a prized prospect at one point and be protected with a 40-man roster spot but at some point the organization feels they have other players they need to protect.

All part of the game.

Chapter 14: May 13 - 17. Away at Mobile BayBears

May 13

The Jumbo Shrimp lost 4-1 to the BayBears and stand at 12-23 on the season, 10 games below .500. It is a testament to his professionalism with Roger Hoover calling these games during this slide. He sees the silver lining in the games. He focuses on the good points.

I'm also down on them right now because I really want to go to a game tonight. I miss seeing live baseball, even if it's only a five or ten game stretch they're on the road.

My career is still a priority, but I've adjusted my schedule to accommodate baseball games into it. There is nothing worse than not having a game to look forward to that night.

Maybe I'll take the wife out for dinner.

Starter Severino Gonzalez took the loss, his third on the season. He gave up all four runs in four innings of work. James Buckelew worked three perfect innings in relief but it was too late. The Jumbo Shrimp bats didn't come alive in this one.

Brian Anderson got the lone Jumbo Shrimp run with a huge homer in the fifth inning.

May 14

A win for the Jumbo Shrimp, breaking their winless streak at six.

Matt Tomshaw got the win. He's now 4-1. He only allowed a run on six hits in 6 ⅔ innings. Ryan Beckman pitched a perfect ninth inning to get his third save.

Alex Yarbrough hit a two-run homer in the third to put the Jumbo Shrimp ahead.

Shortstop Yefri Perez was outrighted to the Jumbo Shrimp and taken off their 40 Man Roster. Hopefully he can get back on the field and start hitting and being a terror on the base paths with his speed.

May 15

Another win for Jacksonville, this time 4-2.

It was a dramatic win, too. With the score tied at two and two outs in the ninth, Alex Glenn hit a two-run homerun. It would be the final score and a big win for the team.

Tyler Higgins got his first win of the season, pitching in relief. Greg Nappo pitched the ninth to get his first save. Joe Gunkel, recently outrighted to the Jumbo Shrimp, pitched a perfect inning.

I'm seeing (hearing since I wasn't actually there but listened in) a few offensive players beginning to get into their groove as the season progresses.

I just hope they can put it all together before the end of the first half of the season.

In the Southern League they play 140 games. A North Division of five teams and South Division of five teams. It is broken into two halves of 70 games, with the winner of each half playing a best of five series to move on. When the winners of these games, the North and South Division Champions, are decided they play in the Southern League Championship.

Right now it's a long-shot the Jumbo Shrimp, in the Southern Division, will make the playoffs as a first half winner.

There were a few roster moves: shortstop Junior Arrojo was brought down from New Orleans. Third baseman Rehiner Cordova was assigned to extended spring training. Catcher Chris Hoo, who can't seem to stay healthy, was placed on the 7-Day DL with a wrist contusion.

And pitcher Raudel Lazo was released.

This one hit home as my wife and I had joined the Booster Club recently and wanted to support a player. It was Raudel.

We joined the booster club and meet the first player we'd be sponsoring, Raudel Lazo. *"For less than a week. We got involved too late to make up his bag for a series of away games. We wanted to meet him. We met him as he was heading to the bus to get on the road with the team. He doesn't speak English very well but we said hello and explained who we were. He was very nice and smiled. Then during the trip he got released by the team. I was also sad because we'd been the first sponsor he'd had for the team. But then, because I can't say no, we ended up sponsoring four more players, making them bags of snacks and drinks for their away games. We always sponsored pitchers, too. Daniel Schlereth, Omar Bencomo and Esmerling De La Rosa,"* my wife said.

May 16th

It was a 4-3 loss for the Jumbo Shrimp. They actually had the lead going into the bottom of the ninth inning, 3-1, but the BayBears rallied for three runs in walk-off fashion.

Reliever Kyle Lobstein took the loss after Ryan Beckman blew the save. It was the seventh blown save for the team so far this year. Not a good sign. They only have eight saves.

Highlights for Jacksonville included a triple by Yefri Perez, who showed his speed. David Vidal also had a triple.

May 17th

In the last game of this series the Jumbo Shrimp took the loss, 9-1. This was yet another road series loss for Jacksonville, who have yet to win a series on the road.

Omar Bencomo, who'd started out strong in the beginning of the year, took another loss. He's now 4-2. He allowed eight runs on eleven hits. Hunter

Adkins pitched three perfect innings in relief but it was already too late.

John Norwood tripled and Cam Maron knocked him in with an RBI single.

Chapter 15: Collecting Baseball Cards

My dad got me into collecting baseball cards. He'd been collecting since he was a kid and when I tell you he has over a million cards it is no exaggeration.

It still is a big bonding thing between us. Since I was born in 1969 I am putting together a 1969 Topps baseball set. One or two cards at a time. I also collect anything Red Sox. The (unrealistic) goal would be to have one of every Red Sox card there is. According to the website I use to collect them, I'm behind. With over 130,000 different Red Sox cards to collect, I've made a very small dent so far. It's not the completion that is the fun, it's adding a card or three here and there and watching me get closer.

Even from an early age I loved studying the stats on the backs of the cards. The history of a player. Where they played before this year. How their career was progressing. Tidbits about each player, too.

During the offseason there wasn't MLB Network and constant baseball news when I was a kid. The only connection to baseball was my card collection. I'd sit in my room and sort the cards by team, putting them in lineup order. Put together the perfect order, knowing when baseball started somehow the manager would unconsciously be fed this vital information from my work and utilize it.

Hey, I was a kid and it was cold outside.

Like I said, my dad had been collecting since he was a kid. I'll let him explain it.

"Back in those days when Topps put out new baseball cards the players would have a stool near their locker. Pete (Sheehy, the clubhouse attendant) would put twenty of a player's card on the stool for him to sign. Pete would take the ones they signed to give out for promotions. Some players didn't sign the cards or only signed a few. My brother would help Pete collect the cards and he got to keep a few. That's when he actually started collecting baseball cards. Before I did. I never took the Yankees cards," my dad told me.

He'd also play a game with the cards.

"When we were kids we'd play against somebody. You'd put down your Cleveland team. Your Boston team. I had a Tigers team. If your player at a position was better than their player you won their card. We'd also flip cards. Bet my team against your team. I started collecting baseball cards in 1960. They were a nickel a pack. Everyone was always looking for that Mantle card. I think it was $1.40 for the box. I remember my buddy Freddy, his father owned a bakery, and he used to get money from his old man for cards. My father never gave me money for them. I never had that dollar to run down to the corner and buy cards. I'd go with Freddy when he'd buy the whole box of cards. Twenty-four packs in the box, each pack had six cards in it. We'd sit in front of

the school and I'd watch him open the packs. He'd take all the gum and put it in his pocket. Maybe give you two pieces. As he opened a pack he'd search for the Yankees cards and toss the rest in a pile. At the end he'd ask if I wanted the non-Yankees cards. Of course I did. I collected a lot of cards as a kid but none of them were Yankees. Now I look back and know how expensive those cards are now and how much they're worth. I'm sure today Freddy is rich off of selling his Yankees cards and I have a roomful of Detroit Tigers cards. We never collected sets. We collected by team to pitch cards. My brother was great at pitching cards. He could throw leaners. I was bad at it. He'd take my cards and go beat other kids with them and win me more cards."

I can see, talking to my dad, how fondly he still remembers being a kid and collecting cards in the beginning.

"In my late teens I stopped collecting. I fell in love with your mother and went to Vietnam. Had you and your brother. In the 70's I started collecting again a little bit and in 1976, when you started being interested in collecting, I jumped back in even more. I would go to baseball card stores during my lunch breaks and buy cards. Between 1976 and 1979 we put sets together. Used the checklist cards to mark off what we had. In 1986 when your grandmother died we were cleaning out her attic, which is where my brother and I used to store our cards. All my cards from the late 1950's and 1960's. I nearly cried when I saw how many of them were damaged from being pitch cards. My collection kept growing and I finally used one of the extra rooms upstairs as my baseball

card room. Before that I had cards everywhere. In the garage. In the closets. Back in the early 1970's I had cards stored at my sister's house because we lived in an apartment and had no room. I had three or four hundred thousand cards at my sister's house. I pulled about a hundred thousand good cards from my mother's attic and added them to my baseball card room, too. I'm amazed her ceiling never caved in with all that weight above our heads. I stopped collecting in 1993 as far as getting modern cards. I'm still collecting but not anything past 1993. In the last twenty-five years I've only collected older cards. I only wanted to collect Topps. I'd go to auctions and buy boxes of mixed cards. There might be ten thousand cards in the box but only two thousand were Topps. I'd keep all the rest in another pile and put together the Topps sets," he said.

For me, it was around 1993 when collecting cards became too much as well. I was in my early twenties and rent and food were the priorities. I'd buy an occasional pack of cards and about once a year I'd go to a baseball card show at the local VFW and spend twenty bucks on complete Red Sox team sets.

I never got rid of any of my cards. When I moved from New Jersey to Florida in 2001 I made sure all of my Red Sox cards came with me.

As my career as a full-time author took off I began slowly collecting more and more cards again. I found a great website that lists every card ever made and I use it as a checklist to fill in my Red Sox and 1969 Topps sets.

130,000 individual cards, just for Red Sox, might seem like a lot. It might be impossible to find them all, even with eBay and so many sellers online.

For me it's not about completing the collection as much as it is finding the rare card I've been searching months for.

I told my wife once the worst thing for me would be to have someone give me all of the Red Sox cards I needed in one shot.

My collection would be complete. I'd be done. I'd be miserable.

Of course, beginning this year I've also started collecting any and all Jacksonville team sets as well. Why not?

Chapter 16: May 18 - 22. Home vs. Mississippi Braves

May 18th

6,071 fans (including me and my wife) saw the Jumbo Shrimp fall short, 6-4 on a Thursday night. The M-Braves first baseman Carlos Franco had three hits, including a fifth-inning grand slam against reliever James Buckelew, who took the loss.

Joe Gunkel looked good until the fifth inning, when he gave up a run and left with the bases loaded. Overall he was hit for four runs on four hits.

In a bunch of roster moves, pitcher Tayron Guerrero was sent down to Jupiter, pitcher Kyle Lobstein moved up to New Orleans along with pitcher Greg Nappo, and pitcher Andy Beltre was promoted from Jupiter along with pitcher Daniel Schlereth.

It looks like the organization is shaking up the minor league pitching staffs to see who can prove they deserve to stay and someday reach the Marlins.

May 19th

Alex Glenn came through again, hitting a ninth inning two-out walk off double and the Jumbo Shrimp got a 5-4 win. 7,437 fans were in attendance for the great finish and fireworks to cap off a solid night of baseball.

Lefty Jeff Locke was on rehab assignment from the Miami Marlins, going 5 ⅓ innings and throwing a lot of strikes. At one point he retired eight batters in a row with four coming on strikeouts.

I need to highlight another player on another team: right fielder Ronald Acuna of the M-Braves. He's on fire since entering the league, currently hitting .415. He had a hit in this game and stole second with ease. My wife laughs because I get so excited to see a player on another team and heap praise on him. Acuna is one of those special players tearing up the Southern League. I want to see him as much as possible because he won't be in Double-A for long.

We were also treated, although since it came against us I guess it wasn't that much of a treat, by an inside the park homerun by M-Braves second baseman Travis Demeritte. Center fielder Yefri Perez misplayed the ball and it got past him.

The newest additions to the Jacksonville pitching staff seem to be a good shot in the arm as Andy Beltre, Ryan Beckman, Daniel Schlereth and Esmerling De La Rosa combined for 3 ⅔ innings. Beckman gave up a double and blew a save opportunity in the seventh inning but then the bullpen shut down the M-Braves to preserve the victory.

My wife hates I say M-Braves constantly. It has a certain ring to it, though. No?

The last three Jumbo Shrimp home wins have been walk-off hits.

May 20th

Here we go again. Right fielder John Norwood hit a walk-off home run in the ninth inning for a 4-3 win over the M-Braves. 7,494 saw the game on Saturday night and the first thousand through the gates received a Jumbo Shrimp hat.

Starter Matt Tomshaw pitched six innings, allowing two earned runs on seven hits. He walked one and struck out six. Severino Gonzalez pitched two perfect innings in relief but righty Andy Beltre blew the save with two outs in the ninth, giving up a solo homer but ending up getting the win thanks to Norwood.

It didn't look good for the Jumbo Shrimp to start the game. Shortstop Alex Yarbrough had a leadoff single but then M-Braves pitcher Wes Parsons retired the next seventeen batters he faced. Yarbrough actually broke the streak with a triple in the sixth.

May 21st

Lefty Mike Kickham not only pitched seven strong innings, he helped his own cause with his first professional home run in a 10-3 win on a Sunday in front of 4,814 fans. He allowed only one run, a solo homer, and scattered three hits. He struck out four.

The Jacksonville bats came alive today. Alex Yarbrough hit his second home run of the season and David Vidal, Cal Towey, Alex Glenn and Yefri Perez collected two hits each for the victory.

May 22nd

Righty Chris Mazza picked up his first win of the season with 5 ⅔ innings as the Jumbo Shrimp continued to win, taking down the M-Braves 5-2 in front of 4,770 on a late Monday morning game. Most of the fans in attendance were students for Education Day.

I was there by myself and made sure to get my souvenir Diet Coke cup and hot dogs before I sat down.

KC Serna and Taylor Ard put on a power display for the kids, both homering. Serna had been in Triple-A the last two weeks and I guess he learned a few things. This was his first Southern League homer, and it came against the M-Braves lefty Max Fried, another guy I've been watching. The Braves minor league system is packed with potential Major League talent and I guarantee Atlanta will be competitive sooner than later.

I got a chance to talk to KC Serna during the season, between him being shuttled back and forth from Double-A to Triple-A.

Going up and down from Jacksonville to New Orleans, how is it mentally as a player?

"It has its highs and lows but ultimately, once you see your name in the lineup, wherever you're at, you just have to compete. If you can master that you'll be alright. Once you stop listening to what people are saying or getting angry over things you can't control, you'll be fine. Once you get in that lineup just do what you do."

Is it easier moving up to Triple-A when you've played with a bunch of those guys already?

"Not really. There are some older guys up there and some guys might get intimidated. When it's all said and done it's just another dude trying to do the same thing you're doing. Some might've been to The Show already but came back down. They might have a bit more experience on you. I don't look at them as someone who might be better than me. He's just another dude trying to do what you're doing."

Besides KC Serna back from New Orleans, shortstop Junior Arrojo was sent down to Jupiter.

Chapter 17: May 24 - 28. Home vs. Jackson Generals

May 24th

The game was postponed due to rain.

I don't like missing games.

I do, however, like chatting with the Jacksonville Jumbo Shrimp manager Randy Ready.

This is your first year in Jacksonville since managing in Jupiter last year. You're familiar with some of these players already. What's the transition for you?

"I've managed at this level before. I don't think it's as big a transition for me as it is for the players. For them it's another stepping stone. Another level of the minor leagues to move up and through. Their goal is to ultimately reach the Major Leagues."

You had a nice Major League career. Do you try to impart the things you've learned and your wisdom to the players or do you let them come to you with questions?

"We cover a lot of things. We play a lot of games so there's a lot to learn. For example, after a home game we have Three Ups and Three Downs. So we cover three positive things that happened over the

course of the game and three negative things. It becomes a teaching moment. All twenty-five players are involved. Everyone contributes. It's so that if one player makes that mistake the other twenty-four don't make the same mistake. In this game there's a lot of trial and error. Those are experiences that happen between the lines. We can only practice so much. Until you actually experience those things over the course of a game, you might not have it sink in. That's the ultimate goal of the training grounds that are the minor leagues. You work at it and recognize it so you don't make basic fundamental mistakes at the Major League level."

How is it now as a former player?

"I try not to forget about how difficult it is. Both offensively and defensively. Since I've already played and at a high level I can help them not make the same mistakes I made through trial and error. The shortcuts I learned and can teach them over the course of thirty-something years in the game. As a coach or manager we give them the information that's accurate but still up to the player to execute it."

You seem to have a lot of fun out there.

"It's baseball. It's not a chemistry test. If you ask anybody who's been in this industry any amount of time they'll tell you not to get too serious. This is a long season and a grind. It's so demanding. You have to keep it fresh. Practice with a purpose but ultimately at game-time, when the lights come on, be ready to compete and put it all out there. You have to have some fun along the way. There are a lot of baseball bloopers and things that happen internally

with travel. In the clubhouse. More than the fan experiences sometimes. It's a serious business but you have to take it light-heartedly, too."

Randy Ready was a pleasure to talk to. He's always got a grin on his face like he's got a joke on the tip of his tongue. Sitting in our seats near the third base line when he's out there coaching third is an added bonus because of his interaction with the crowd and the players and umpires.

May 25th

Lefty Jeff Locke, making his second rehab start for the Jumbo Shrimp, went six shutout innings and Omar Bencomo, Severino Gonzalez and Tyler Higgins each pitched a scoreless inning for a 5-0 win in front of 5,481 on a Thursday night.

The Jumbo Shrimp did it on the hitting side, too. They had eight hits, including two by KC Serna, and made the most of it by scoring five runs.

The Jumbo Shrimp need more wins like this with balanced pitching and hitting. A few of the batters are under the Mendoza Line, which is not good.

The Mendoza Line refers to shortstop Mario Mendoza, a journeyman shortstop that played from 1974 until 1982 for three teams. He was always at or near a .200 batting average and his teammates would make fun of him. One time they made fun of superstar George Brett of Kansas City because he'd gotten off to a slow start, warning him not to sink below the Mendoza Line. Brett mentioned it to ESPN's Chris Berman, who started using it during

Sportscenter and it stuck. Ironically, Mario ended his career with a .215 average, above the Mendoza Line.

May 26th

Let's play two.

In game one the Jumbo Shrimp came down from a 5-0 deficit with eight runs in the fifth inning to win 9-5. They took the second game in easier fashion with a 6-2 win.

The pair of victories gives the Jumbo Shrimp (now 22-26 on the season) seven straight wins on a Friday night in front of 5,731 fans.

Joe Gunkel started game one and allowed the five runs on seven hits. He went 4 ⅔ innings before righty Esmerling De La Rosa came on, giving up a single before getting a strikeout to end the inning. Esmerling picked up the victory and Daniel Schlereth pitched the last two innings without giving up a run to get the save.

The personal hitting highlight was third baseman Brian Anderson hitting his seventh homer of the season. I'm starting to see a race between Anderson and Norwood for the team home run crown.

In the second game starter Matt Tomshaw (now 5-1) went six, only allowing two earned runs and five hits. He struck out five, too.

Catcher Cam Maron hit a homer and John Norwood had two RBI's in each game today.

May 27th

Lefty Mike Kickham had twelve strikeouts in 6 ⅔ scoreless innings but then the relievers let it slip away, with Andy Beltre giving up two runs in an inning of work and Severino Gonzalez pitching 1 ⅓ innings, also giving up two runs and not only blowing the save but getting the loss.

The loss snapped the Jacksonville seven game winning streak.

John Norwood hit his eighth home run of the season.

I had a chance to ask John a few questions during the season. Here's one of them.

You're hitting some homers so far this year. Is that the goal, John?

"The power just comes with it. I try to hit line drives. Every time I try to hit a homerun I roll over or foul it off. The power numbers are there but it isn't what I'm trying to do. The goal is to make hard contact. Be as successful as I can with that because the goal is getting a hit. Getting on base. Not always trying for the homer but making solid contact and getting hits. That's what you get paid for," the quiet Norwood told me.

David Vidal was promoted to New Orleans as catcher Chris Hoo was activated from the disabled list.

May 28th

6,290 fans on a partly cloudy mid-90's day saw a 5-1 loss in the series finale.

Chris Mazza got the loss. He's now 1-3. He went six innings and gave up three runs on six hits. He struck out two.

The Jumbo Shrimp had ten hits on the day but it only amounted to one run.

It feels like the brief momentum they had on their winning streak has now been taken away. Tomorrow is a travel day as they start a series in Pensacola. I'm hoping they can win a few games and get their mojo back.

My wife and I are excited because we'll get to see the last two games in Pensacola.

Chapter 18: Jumbo Shrimp Staff Interviews

When I first had the idea for this book I knew without even a little bit of help from the team it would go nowhere. I'd written nonfiction books before, interviewing women in heavy metal as well as a book about a local Orlando-based pro wrestling company. Both times I had full support of those I was interviewing as well as management.

It's very important. I've had a couple of ideas for books over the years that went nowhere because I couldn't get the important people to give me any access or be available for my questions.

The Jumbo Shrimp went out of their way to help me. Above and beyond. Access to players and the staff as well as being able to watch batting practice and wander the stadium before a game.

It starts with Noel Blaha, who was immediately onboard when I explained my vision for the book. I conducted several interviews with some of the office staff, giving me an inside look at the day-to-day workings of the team.

I hope these interviews will also give you some insight as well.

Noel Blaha, Assistant GM

What's your normal day-to-day during a home game?

"Helping to make sure everything is running smoothly. The departments I directly oversee are media relations, in marketing as well as on-field promotions. Also the merchandise department. I need to make sure everything is set to go. The people that report to me are really, really good. I'm more or less helping them put out fires as they pop up. I make sure our plan is in place to attack each homestand so we're prepared and ready to go."

How does it differ when the team is on the road?

"When the team is on the road it's more out of sight out of mind. Initially. But we're always planning two weeks ahead. If the team is out of town tomorrow we're planning for the next homestand. Make sure we're staffed properly. Promotions are in place. We have to make sure everything is ready in advance. When the team is out of town you can breathe a little bit. There's less foot traffic through the offices, but with the new merchandise and better ticket sales we're still seeing a lot more people than before. Personally it's great because I get to go home and have dinner with my family. That can be a challenge during ten-game home stands."

With the name change and the new merchandising, were you expecting this much in merch sales or was it a pleasant surprise?

"We were definitely expecting an increase in attention. The sales and the amount of repeat customers exceeded our expectations. I was blown

away. We made the name change and the merchandise was flying off the shelves. Not only nationally with online sales but the foot traffic in The Baseball Grounds was really high. What I was really blown away by was the amount of people who showed up on Opening Day already in their gear and ready to go buy more. The brand really resonates with people. It's a multi-pronged thing. People say we changed the name to sell some shirts. Well, kind of. You don't buy a new house just for the garage or the kitchen. All of that plays into it. The tangible thing that people see extends the Crustacean Nation feeling."

Spring training. How do you prepare?

"The team stuff itself we have no say in whatsoever. We don't get tied down in the day to day minutia of who's going to be the first baseman. We might know the manager before spring training but sometimes it's not until a few days in. The team on the field is out of our hands. We're more concerned with the sponsorship deals, the ballpark is clean and ready to go, and on the merchandise side of things making sure we have enough in stock and we have it planned out when things are going to arrive."

Was there a huge increase in news media with the name change?

"Yes. Coming to Jacksonville when I did, after the 2015 season, I was really excited about the challenge of working in an NFL market. We share a parking lot area with the Jaguars. I was interested in the challenge of how to get people's attention in a market that already has an NFL team. With not only the name change but the business model we implemented, we were getting the attention not only

from the sports columnists and beat writers but in the business section. That's important to us. We want to grow what affordable family fun is. To be able to get the attention of the business folks first was important because of our change to the business model. The structure of what baseball was at The Baseball Grounds. As we went into year two with a name change, we were getting the attention of even more people. The lifestyle section. We did a fashion show with First Coast News. There are so many different avenues so the people aren't just looking at us as a professional baseball team. They look at us as a fashion icon. A year-round business."

How has Ken Babby and his team made a difference?

"Ken is one of the main reasons I left Charleston. A place I'd been for ten seasons. I was very comfortable there and it was a great ownership group, too. Ken's vision of creating affordable family fun and excitement around the baseball games was really something that attracted me personally. I think the community is reaping the benefits of his vision and his energy. You sit down with him for a couple of minutes and he goes a million miles a minute. He's always bringing such energy. Being able to work hand in hand with Ken on some of these things with The Baseball Grounds and the Jumbo Shrimp has been really, really exciting."

You have the Jaguars in your back parking lot. Across the street at the arena the Sharks and IceMen play. How do you look at that?

"We don't view those other sports teams in town as competition. We're all in it together. The Jaguars

is a completely different beast. We have excellent relationships with the Jaguars. Excellent with the Armada, the Sharks, and the IceMen as well. We view ourselves as an entertainment option. Our competition isn't necessarily another sports team. It's more the beach. Good restaurants. Different family activities. We segment ourselves with those other teams. We're lucky to have such great working relationships with all those teams. A strong sports scene in Jacksonville benefits all the teams."

How many new people did Ken bring in when he took over the team?

"Initially about five people stayed on from the previous ownership. At this point a few of those people have moved on so it's down to two that have stayed on. Brian DeLettre, the Creative Services Manager, and Theresa Viets, our Military Liaison."

How many people had you worked with previously?

"I worked with Harold Craw. We worked for eight seasons together in Charleston. Linda McNabb worked for the ownership group for Charleston. We'd done sales training and things like that together. Ashley McCallen is our Sales & Marketing Coordinator. Birthday parties and corporate sales. She was actually an intern for us in Charleston. We all worked together and then under the Fast Forward Sports umbrella the GM of Akron, Jim Pfander, was also the President of Fast Forward Sports, which is Ken's group. In 2008 in Charleston I was the box office manager, Harold was Director of Sales, Jim was the Assistant GM, Akron's Assistant GM Scott Riley was the Merchandise Director in Charleston.

It's a network. In minor league baseball everybody knows everybody. It's like coaching circles. Who you feel comfortable with."

Harold Craw, General Manager

A few of you came over after previously working together. How was the transition?

"It was good, which is the quick answer. It was an opportunity to do what a lot of organizations might not do, which was being able to build a front office with guys who have experiences in other markets. Honestly, it was not that difficult because I already had a relationship with the majority of the people here. Ultimately, once those people that you know are in place, you try to figure out what type of personality you want to fill out the rest of the spots with."

You've moved up the ladder in minor league baseball.

"I started as a sales manager in Charleston in '04. It was an opportunity to work for one of the premier organizations at that time. Work for a baseball maverick in Mike Veek, too. Being able to be involved in some promotional meetings where there were some random things tossed around the room was great. We had Silent Night. It was the most silent game on record. Everyone there signed a banner and shipped it to the Guiness Book of World Records. Being involved in baseball and watching the evolution of the Yankees minor league system become a part of Charleston was pretty cool. Saw a lot of

guys that are now in the big leagues. One of the highlights for me was a chance to be there when we hosted the All-Star Game and did a Home Run Derby off a battleship. Despite what anyone else in minor league baseball may say or do, Bill Murray was the brainchild of that along with Noel Blaha."

Working with such an iconic promotions family, do you take some of that with you for the future?

"The philosophy that there's no such thing as a bad idea. A lot of it is how it evolves. You try it out. Sometimes it doesn't work so you move it to the left or to the right. I think it's what makes us such a unique group here. Everyone has different ideas. They've seen them in previous stops from different parts of the country. Jacksonville is a very eclectic place, with people from different areas. It's pretty cool to be able to put our ideas together. Mike Veek tried to do some ridiculous things. He tried to be as outside of the box as possible. We're thinking about what we can do inside the baseball park."

What's your daily routine when the team is home?

"Making sure everything is under control for tonight's game. If it's a non-game day talking with our management staff is a big part of it, and meeting with anyone who has questions. And just like anyone else in the sales office, I'm a sales guy. A lot of it is corporate relationships we currently have in place. Mine are probably a little different than others. I'm just as much a front office employee as everyone else."

What's your daily relationship with the Marlins?

"Much more after the season. Last year when we were at the end of the player developmental contract, we had conversations on a daily basis to come up with an agreement for how long we were going to extend it. Normally it's just emails back and forth. Most are just basic questions, or if there's someone coming into town that needs a room. Probably the most interaction, not even so much with the Marlins, this year our play by play announcer Roger Hoover is doing a lot of the stuff with guys being sent down or brought up. Making sure they have a hotel room. He's taken over that process. Which is great, because he's on the bus with these guys. He's with them twenty-four hours a day. When the phone rings and someone is coming Roger can handle it. I'd like to say our relationship with the Marlins is fantastic. They want to chat for five or ten minutes when they're in town. They want to know if we need anything."

You have no say in roster moves.

"My job is more like running a small business. It's just cool to be around some of the guys and see them coming through the system and stopping in Jacksonville along the way. I tell people it's why they pay scouts to come down and look at talent. I have no eye for talent, nor would I want to do that part of it. There are too many things that hinge on the success of a guy that has nothing to do with physical talent. His raw psyche. The kind of person they're going to be in a pressure situation. A lot of talent scouting is just talking to the guy. A lot of times we interact with former players, too. Guys who might be in their late 50's or early 60's. Traveling through, whether they're a special assistant or scouting. That's pretty

cool. To be able to see a guy like Andre Dawson, who is one of my heroes? He's now a special assistant with the Marlins. When the Mississippi Braves come to town, generally, Bobby Cox will be around. He doesn't live too far from here. We get a lot of visitors. We even had Tony LaRussa in the ballpark. That's pretty cool for me because these are the players and managers I followed growing up. I'm a huge Braves fan. I grew up about ninety miles north of Atlanta in Chattanooga Tennessee. Every Sunday I would watch the Braves with my dad and my grandfather. We'd go to my grandparent's house and have dinner there. I was a fan before they became a successful ballclub. Watching them as an organization improve was cool. As a fan watching how they put those teams together. It's one of the things that got me interested in the game."

Linda McNabb, Vice President of Sales & Marketing

What is your job specifically?

"Anything that has to do with revenue. Oversight with Noel when it comes to marketing and the customer service with the team."

You were the first hire for the new group when they came in?

"I was. Ken's partner, Jim in Akron, as well as Harold and Noel all worked together in a sports group in our past. I came here from Ft. Myers Miracle, a Single-A team. We all worked for the group that owned the team. We all kept in touch but

went our own way but we kept in touch. When Jim and Ken bought the Akron team they flew me up. They wanted me to work for them. I'm originally from Cleveland. I fell in love with the ballpark. It was the first time I'd ever met Ken. Had great respect for Jim. I loved everything they talked about but couldn't get past the fact it was November and about thirty-nine degrees. Not cold enough to snow but it rained from the moment I got off until I got back on the plane. I declined the offer but told them if you ever head south please let me know. Fast forward four years later and I get the call from Jim again saying they were getting closer to me. They wanted to talk to me again. How close? We started talking in October of 2014. I didn't know specifically it was Jacksonville at the time. Once I knew where it was I came up a couple of times. Because I'd been in baseball for fifteen years I knew who Peter "Pedro" Bragan Jr., the old owner, was. I knew Chris Peters, who was the general manager. He actually worked for me in Fort Myers and left there to come here. I knew who they were but nothing about the team. I started July 1st of 2015. Before we actually got the team. Took it over. My job was to come into town and assess. Sit back. Be quiet. I came to a lot of games. Always incognito with the hat, the sunglasses and a little pad of paper. Trying to figure out who were their sponsors. It was my job to start putting together a plan. We knew it was probably going to come with some challenges in the beginning. You had an owner that was family for over thirty years. Very cemented in the community. There weren't issues with branding. Everyone in town knew who the Suns were."

How did the name change affect you?

"Not too long after we changed the name I asked Ken if we could have a year where there aren't going to be any major changes. Speaking for me, I don't think I anticipated the boisterous negative reaction we got. I wasn't sure if people would care one way or the other. It was just a name. It wasn't most people, luckily. But the ones who were negative seemed loud. The first time I saw the logo I immediately fell in love with the colors and logos. This team needed the next chapter. I think when we came in and Ken bought the team we started to think of what we could do to make an immediate impact. One of the things we all noticed immediately was all it would take would be some very minor changes. A couple of things we noticed right away like the logo looking tired. That was the feel we took away from the beginning, even before we took over. It wasn't that the logo itself was bad. It was just very old school. This is a great ballpark with great fans. A great team on the field. All these elements were awesome. It wasn't in line with minor league baseball today with the name and logo. We felt it was an easy fix. You inject some enthusiasm into this and remind all of the staff that the first thing you need to do at the gate is to smile. Just smile. Welcome people. That's why we're here. From the Marlins standpoint this is all about player development but from our point of view it's all about the fans. To be frank, there weren't that many coming in the old days. We wanted to zap the community and get the mojo going. The first step is thanking them for coming. That doesn't cost anything. We also cleaned. Smile and clean and you've made an impression. In the beginning it was

about the minor changes that we needed to make. We needed to invigorate the community again. Ken did a lot of appearances and we all went into the community every chance we got. We also had to find out what the community really felt about the Suns. How did it translate into putting butts in seats? And what do we need to do to get more butts in seats?"

What about fans still insisting they're still the Suns?

"I welcome them. If you want to wear your Suns stuff, come on. It's okay. It's fine. But come. Enjoy. Because you're going to find out the name has changed but what else has changed is a positive. You'll see it's a cleaner ballpark. There's more energy now. We're very careful about who we hire. Whether we're talking about an usher, a corporate salesperson, a group sales guy or whoever. The ticket takers. You have to want to be here. We want you here and we want you to come back so we need to make sure you have a good time. Wear your Suns stuff all day long. We'll keep winning goofy promotions of the year and getting national attention for Jacksonville."

Once the season ends, what changes for you?

"I get busier once the season ends. We've already started the planning for 2018. We make assessments on everything, so we go back through every piece of inventory we have, every ticket that we have. Does it work or do we leave it alone? Figure out what we need to tweak or when we need to add something. We've already started to do all of that. We start budgeting, figuring out if we need more people in the community. Are we good with what we have as

far as the numbers go? Another big part for us on the management side is mentoring. Coaching is a huge part of it. Some of them want to be a GM. Others want to move up and into the majors. Maybe they want to try a different sport. That's also part of what we do. After the season ends is all an assessment time. We need to figure out how to do things better. We want to be the leading group so teams in other cities look to us to find out what we're doing and what we're doing right. All of us work very well together as a team. And then we start selling again. That starts right away with either getting our partners renewed or bringing new people into the fold. Start selling season tickets again."

Brennan Earley, Merchandise Manager

Describe your job.

"In-season I manage the online store during the day. We almost always have online orders. I'll go ahead and process those first. I do everything from listing the item on the website to checking the inventory to pulling the order from the store to packaging. Then ship it out. I also have to do the inventory for the store, which is done on a daily basis. If items are coming in I have to process them and get them to the floor as soon as possible, especially if it's an item we're currently low or out of. I have to deal with the invoices and setting everything in the store on the racks."

How much input do you have on the items you're stocking?

"All of it. That leads us to the offseason. I start about two weeks after the season ends; I've already started on some of it. I'll dedicate a week where I'm doing hats. I'll go through the hat companies, their catalogues, and pick out some new items that catch my eye. What I think might work here. Then I reach out to the reps from each company. Most of them have a rep dedicated to Florida because of so many teams. I'll tell them which hats I'm looking at and then customize it how I would like it to look. They'll mock up and artwork and send it back. If it's great I'll approve it. I can put an order in for it. If not we'll edit it until it is right. Once my hat order is done I'll spend the next week on novelty items. It's a smaller category. I usually try to save men's and women's because it's the two biggest categories. They take the longest. That takes me from mid-September all the way into April and May. With some companies they want you to start working for the following season in July. I've already started doing some hats. I won't claim credit for all the merchandise we did. Some of it came from Noel. We bounce around ideas when we have our promotional meetings. With ordering shirts, there's so much to choose from. Styles of the shirts, artwork for them. I might like the concept they started but need to make it more in line with what we could sell. It's not rocket science but it's more than just slapping a logo on a shirt."

What was the challenge for you with the changing of the team name?

"Getting items in as quickly as possible. Harold called me into his office and let me know about the change. He gave me the logos and the colors I needed

to start ordering stuff. We did that about a week after the Suns season had ended. I had to sign a non-disclosure. I couldn't tell anyone. Only a few people in the office knew about the change. I couldn't sit at my normal desk to do orders. They had me in the press box by myself ordering. The biggest challenge was making sure by November 2nd when we launched the name we had something to sell. We knew we'd get backlash for the name but there'd also be the flipside with people loving the change and wanting merchandise immediately. The immediate problem was hats. The shirts we could get done fast no matter what company we used. Hats were another story, especially with New Era, who is the official on-field hats company. It was a struggle with them because normally you need three months once you place the order. The biggest problem was that we only received 144 of each hat when we launched. That's not nearly enough. We sold out of them in about a day. We had no more fitted hats. The next shipment didn't come in until the week before Christmas. We're also taking online orders, too, so they were being backordered. We had a massive backorder list of people waiting on hats. I'm the one who has to fulfill all of them when the hats finally arrive. We had people coming in every day asking when the hats were going to get here. They told me the hats would be back in stock the end of November. Then they told me the first week of January. It finally showed up the week before Christmas which was just around the time we'd opened the store. We had remodeled and renovated it with the new name and colors. It was a madhouse. We had two people staying in the store because of a constant stream of people coming in to buy merchandise. Two or three of us in the office for the online fulfillment. We had one person just making priority mail boxes. Stack them. Someone else would print up the orders. I was putting it all together and taping it up. Once we got the inventory in it got a lot smoother. The initial problem was just getting the stuff in. After January the main orders start coming in. it begins relieving the pressure. We only had four or five shirts in the beginning. We only had four or five hats. Those were constantly being hit by everyone. Once the other stuff started coming in people started buying other stuff as well so sales dropped off on the original items enough we could keep up with demand."

Were you surprised with the initial amount of orders?

"Oh, yeah. No one expected it to be like this. It's been wild. You see it everywhere. I'm not just talking local, either. We've seen it on Twitter with someone wearing Jumbo Shrimp merchandise at the U.S. Open. Someone saw it on TV and took a screenshot. The guy whose photo was taken found out about it and reached out to us. It's been crazy. We didn't expect the exposure. We've been on ESPN a bunch of times when they were talking about the name change. In Sports Illustrated *they mentioned it. People love the logos, too. They might not even care about the team as much as they want to wear the logo in some cases. The colors and the actual logo is all it takes."*

Where are you shipping to?

"About two weeks after the launch we had shipped to all fifty states. Even now about six out of

every ten orders aren't local. A ton to Los Angeles and to Seattle, which was surprising. It's almost as far away as you can get from Jacksonville in the continental United States. New York and the Northeast are always being shipped to as well as the D.C. area. A lot of fans in Akron ordered stuff, which is Ken's other team. I get a lot of random ones. Yesterday I shipped to Fargo North Dakota. England orders started coming in, which I have a feeling was because of the connection with the Jaguars. Then it started branching out to Spain and France. Germany and Italy. New Zealand and Japan. Then Australia."

Ken Babby, Owner of *Your* Jacksonville Jumbo Shrimp

Why baseball for you?

"I grew up around the game. My father was General Counsel to the Baltimore Orioles. I grew up going to games with him. Spending time at the ballpark. After school he'd pick me up. We'd drive up to Oriole Park at Camden Yards. He wouldn't let me out of his office until my math homework was done. When it was I could sit with him and watch games. I remember, from my earliest days, just being around the ballpark. My spring break meant I was usually at Spring Training. It's been a lot of fun. This in some ways has been an evolution. Never in my life would I dream I'd be in a situation to run not one but two teams. I'm first and foremost a huge baseball fan."

How did you get into owning a baseball team?

"Sometimes it comes out of left field. I spent about fourteen years of my life at The Washington Post in a variety of different media roles. Spent time in technology and the company's digital business with sales and marketing operations as the Chief Revenue Officer for the company. When I left the Post in 2012 I was in a situation where I wanted to figure out what to do next. My real passion was still baseball. I started traveling the summers, looking at minor league teams around the country. Trying to understand what the issues were. How someone would be able to get involved in the business. I discovered a small town in Ohio, Akron, where the baseball team was for sale. They were known as the Akron Aeros then, the Double-A affiliate of the Cleveland Indians. I bought the team and moved to Akron. Really imbedded ourselves in the community. Rebranded the team the Rubber Ducks in 2014. It's been really well-received by the community there. The rest is history."

Were you always a fan of minor league baseball?

"Yeah, I always loved minor league baseball because I felt it was all about fan experience. It's certainly about the game on the field but as the owner of the team I can't control the players on the field. I can tell you a lot about the food we have in the ballpark. The cost of tickets. What promotions we have tonight. Great activities for kids like letting them play catch on the field before the game. Like you, I'm a fan and I'll watch until the end of the game. Root our team on to victory. You wouldn't want me as the owner walking down to Randy Ready's office telling him who to pitch tonight."

Were you aware when you came into Akron about the lack of control with the team on the field?

"This business is about understanding the nuances of what we do well and what we have the opportunity to grow. Other opportunities and there's room for us to expand. I think we felt first and foremost that with minor league baseball we could emphasize the great fan experience. The food. The fireworks. The promotions. If we can do it and also get lucky and have a good team on the field it would be a great product for people."

The frustration must be not being able to control the game itself, though.

"You can't build this on the baseball team. You build it on the experience. We know that our food is going to be great. We know our promotions are awesome. Activities for kids are great. We know the pricing is going to be affordable. We know a family of four can come down here for twenty bucks and have a great time. There aren't too many things you can do for twenty bucks, right? Those are the things we focus on. Things that we can control."

Did you take the blueprint you had put together in Akron and bring it here?

"We did. We have a great management team who understands what they key elements are for our fans. Every year, when the season ends, we'll catch our breath. We'll sit down and think about what we can do in 2018 to make this operation shine. Last year, coming out of that meeting, it was all about the name change. This year we won't change the name again. I promise you that. We'll have a couple of other fun tricks up our sleeve."

What is your relationship with the Marlins organization?

"We have a player development contract with them. They control everything on the field, from the players to the coaches. We take care of the team's travel. Hotels. Help out with some lodging. Other than that, not much. They control the baseball side. We don't interfere in their world. I don't tell them how to fill out a lineup card and they don't tell us what to charge for a hot dog. They're two dollars every game, by the way. You can't complain about that, right? It works out well."

My wife and I joke it is cheaper coming here for a night out than anywhere else.

"We want people to feel that way. We actually want you to leave here and feel like you had a great affordable experience. You can go home with some money still in your wallet. That's a very important thing. It also hopefully makes you want to come back for more."

You're very hands-on to the point you're on the field tossing t-shirts into the crowd during the game.

"That started four or five years ago in Akron. It was a dreary Tuesday night in April. Very cold temperatures. Not the kind of night you dream about in minor league baseball. We were short a couple of interns that night. I was down in the tunnel and somebody asked if anyone wanted to toss shirts. I said I'd do it. I grabbed a bag of t-shirts and went out on the field. I had the greatest time of my life. It gives me a special connection with our fans. When I'm in either ballpark I want to be out there with our fans. You know, the winter is long. All of us baseball fans

know how long those six months can be without the crack of the bat or the snap of the ball caught by a glove. I just love being around the game. If I throw a t-shirt to a young kid he or she will remember that for the rest of his life. It's something I take very seriously."

What's the offseason like for you?

"The core planning and strategic work for our company is done during the offseason. A lot of our sales work is done during the offseason as well. The planning of every home game promotional night, figuring out what new food items to include, working through special promotions we're planning, those things are all thought out during those dreary December and January months. By the time February and March come around we have an exciting promotional schedule. We try to build this excitement every year by late February or early March. Fans want to see the promotional schedule. What are the giveaways going to be? We work really hard on that. I also spend a lot of time doing community appearances. We've made over three hundred appearances as an organization in the past year. That might be at a Kiwanis Club or charity groups. Bringing Southpaw and Scampi out to a library to be able to meet with kids. We take what we do really seriously. I want to be able to make sure we're doing it the right way."

Chapter 19: May 30 - June 3. Away vs. Pensacola Blue Wahoos

May 30th

Yesterday the team made a couple of moves, promoting righty Hunter Adkins to New Orleans and swapping him for lefty Chris O'Grady.

Jacksonville lost, 6-0. Omar Bencomo went three innings and gave up a run on two hits but walked four for the loss. He's now 4-3.

Apparently yesterday's roster moves didn't stick because Hunter Adkins was back and gave up three earned runs in two innings.

Jacksonville only managed three hits on the night. Austin Nola had two and John Norwood got the other one.

Pitcher Chris O'Grady was sent back to New Orleans, pitcher Ryan Beckman was shipped to Jupiter and righty Tayron Guerrero promoted from Jupiter.

I love these chess-piece roster moves.

My wife? Not so much.

May 31st

The Jumbo Shrimp got the win tonight by a narrow 9-8 margin after a thirty minute rain delay. Starter Joe Gunkel went four innings, allowing six runs on six hits. Severino Gonzalez earned the win with two scoreless innings to end the game.

Alex Yarbrough was the deciding factor as he went 4-for-5, including a solo home run in the top of the ninth to give his team the lead.

KC Serna and Cal Towey also hit homers.

June 1st

Pensacola won, 5-2, and beat starter Matt Tomshaw. He falls to 5-2 on the year. He went six innings but gave up four runs. He had six strikeouts.

Highlights for Jacksonville were KC Serna hitting another homer tonight, his third on the season, and Brian Anderson, John Norwood and Jeremias Pineda each getting two hits.

June 2nd

The wife and I were at this game. She has to run up to Atlanta every month for work, and I sometimes take the ride with her. We decided to head to Pensacola instead of right back to Jacksonville and catch a couple of ballgames. Check out Blue Wahoos Stadium.

We bought seats right behind the Jumbo Shrimp dugout, roughly where our seats are at the Baseball Grounds. Wearing our Jumbo Shrimp gear, we stuck out but the fans were nice. The usher asked us a lot of questions.

Randy Ready, coaching third base, looked confused when he heard cheering in the stands for the visiting team. He looked right at us and squinted before shaking his head.

Plus, as a bonus, we saw our team win, 7-2. Mike Kickham, the Southern League Pitcher of the Week, pitched seven innings and only allowed one run on four hits. He walked one and struck out four. The losing pitcher was Deck McGuire (again… such a baseball player name).

Timely hitting was also the key to this win. Yefri Perez had an RBI triple in the second inning. His speed is amazing. Austin Nola had a homerun and Brian Anderson added a two-run triple as well. Then he followed it up with a two-run homer in the seventh.

Esmerling De La Rosa worked the last two innings.

We had a great time and can't wait for tomorrow night as well.

June 3rd

It was another loss for the Jumbo Shrimp and another series loss as well. They're now winless in six tries in a road series.

Our seats tonight were down the third base line close to the Jumbo Shrimp bullpen. Once again the people around us asked a lot of questions and were humored we'd come so far to see a game.

My wife went over to the bullpen and introduced herself before the game, especially to the players we were currently sponsoring with goodies and drinks for road trips: Esmerling De La Rosa, Daniel Schlereth, Omar Bencomo and Andy Beltre. They were all very nice and appreciative of us putting the bags together for the road trips.

The weather wasn't cooperating. It was cold, windy and raining off and on the entire game. They kept playing and we kept watching.

We sat in the second row and the guy in front of us was obviously a regular. He started questioning why we were there and why we rooted for the Jumbo Shrimp, messing around with us. It was a good-natured ribbing back and forth the entire game.

At one point his wife took out her Yankees umbrella. I leaned forward and showed the guy my Red Sox phone case and he laughed and started goofing on me even more.

Unfortunately, he also kept looking back and shaking his head whenever the Jumbo Shrimp made an error.

They made seven tonight. Two errors shy of the league record. I can only imagine how much more fun the guy in front of me would've had if that had been the case.

They lost 11-6, too. Another road series loss.

There were a couple of highlights on the field for the Jumbo Shrimp. John Norwood hit a three-run homer. Yefri Perez hit another triple.

Because of all the errors starter Chris Mazza ended with a no-decision and none of the four runs were earned.

Despite the loss we enjoyed the stadium and the game. Our goal in the next couple of seasons is to visit all of the stadiums in the Southern League and catch the Jumbo Shrimp as a visitor.

It was back to the hotel to get some sleep because we'd need to drive home in the morning. We had the start of another homestand to attend.

Chapter 20: June 4 - 8. Home vs. Montgomery Biscuits

June 4th

Our good friends Shawn and Warren surprised us by purchasing the two seats next to us. It made my wife especially happy, since I can sometimes get so mesmerized by a game I won't talk for several innings. Watching a live baseball game is the only place I can stop worrying about writing, bills, my weight and anything else for awhile.

The four of us got to see a 5-2 loss for Jacksonville. Starter James Buckelew, now 0-4 on the season, went four innings and allowed three runs on five hits.

Third baseman Brian Anderson hit his ninth home run of the season and had two RBI's. He is tied for the RBI lead in the league with 38.

June 5th

It was a smaller Monday night crowd tonight. 2,258 in attendance. So far this season the Jumbo Shrimp had been at or near the top in attendance in the Southern league, a testament to the team, both on and off the field, putting together the home games with excitement for the crowds.

Another loss didn't help, either.

Starter Joe Gunkel (now 0-2) went five innings and gave up three runs. Reliever Andy Beltre had an off night, as he gave up a triple and then a wild pitch. He allowed one earned run on two hits and two walks. Esmerling De La Rosa pitched two innings but gave up another run on two hits. Tyler Higgins pitched a scoreless ninth.

I have to point out another great player on an opposing team: Braxton Lee. Tonight he went 2-for-5 and he's hitting .320. In the first he had a single and stole second. I like to watch at least one guy on each team and Lee is definitely the standout for the Biscuits.

Shortstop KC Serna was promoted to New Orleans. Third baseman Rehiner Cordova was added to the Jumbo Shrimp from extended spring training.

June 6th

It was a dreary Tuesday night at the Baseball Grounds. After nearly an hour rain delay the game started. I wish they hadn't gotten this one in, because it ended up being another loss for the Jumbo Shrimp.

The Biscuits had sixteen hits in the 9-3 win. Only two of their hitters didn't get a hit.

Lefty Matt Tomshaw went five innings, giving up six runs on ten hits. Hunter Adkins gave up a run in three innings of relief and Tayron Guerrero gave up two runs in an inning of mop-up duty.

Alex Yarbrough hit his fourth homer of the season and Alex Glenn had his third. Glenn is a player my wife really likes. He always has a smile on his face. I'm hoping he can rebound and start hitting again. He's one of the guys under the Mendoza Line.

Starter James Buckelew was assigned to extended spring training. First baseman Cal Towey was promoted to New Orleans. Righty Clayton Mortensen was promoted from Batavia to Jacksonville. Shortstop Chris Diaz, a recent signing from the Pirates organization, was assigned to the Jumbo Shrimp.

June 7th

It rained. A lot. The game was postponed. There would be a doubleheader tomorrow. Hoping the break lets the Jumbo Shrimp players regroup and get some rest.

June 8th

Jacksonville came away with a split of the doubleheader, both games seven-inning contests in front of 4,972 fans.

In game one, a 3-2 loss, starter Chris Mazza took the loss. He went five innings but gave up three runs on eleven hits. Righty Clayton Mortensen made his Jumbo Shrimp debut and pitched a scoreless inning.

Daniel Schlereth finished with a scoreless inning of his own but it was too late.

Center fielder Jeremias Pineda went 3-for-3, raising his average to .244. He's beginning to hit the ball and hit it well.

Lefty starter Mike Kickham, one of the Jacksonville All-Star representatives, pitched a complete game shutout in a seven-inning second game.

This 1-0 win was a pitching gem. The Jumbo Shrimp only managed two hits, a single by Alex Yarbrough and Brian Anderson's tenth home run of the season. Anderson will also be a Southern League All-Star along with Kickham and pitcher Matt Tomshaw and outfielder John Norwood.

If Anderson keeps hitting the way he's hitting he'll be sent to New Orleans before the end of the season.

Chapter 21: Mark Fidrych

Friday. May 27th. 1977.

We drove from New Jersey to Detroit because Mark 'The Bird' Fidrych was back.

"He had been hurt in spring training in '77. Hurt his knee while shagging fly balls. Fidrych had to have surgery and was out. I couldn't wait to see him pitch again," my dad said.

My mother takes over the story. *"Your father had been waiting for Fidrych to come back. Next month? Next week? Then he got word he was pitching Friday night, which was the next day. He woke me up and told me to get dressed, pack some clothes and wake up you and your brother. We were heading to Detroit."*

"Back in '77 there was no all-day sports channels. You had to listen to the AM radio for sports breaks or watch the 5 o'clock news for their five minutes of sports, which was usually about the Yankees or Mets. When I found out he was coming back and starting I knew there was no way I was missing it," my dad said. *"It was a night game so we had to leave super early to get there on time. I think we pulled into the parking lot in the afternoon and waited for the game to start."*

I remember my brother getting a nosebleed. He always got a nosebleed as a kid. No matter where we went it seemed like the faucet was turned on and he'd be covered in blood. It's probably why seeing blood makes me pass out now.

"We walked up and got tickets. We sat as far away in the stadium as you could. It didn't matter. We were just excited to be there to see him pitch," my mom said.

My dad is smiling as he remembers the game like it was last year and not forty years ago. *"It was a good game. He always put on a show when he pitched. We were way out in left field. Pitcher Dave Rozema came out and was throwing balls into the crowd. It was wild. The crowd was wild. After the game we got a hotel outside of Detroit. At the time we loved spur of the moment trips like that. We all loved baseball so it was a fun family adventure."*

It doesn't even matter that Fidrych lost, 2-1 that night. The crowd of 44,207 cheered for him with every pitch. Every time he talked to the ball.

He gave up two runs, only one of them earned. Gave up eight hits and one walk. Struck out three.

The Bird pitched a complete game in his first start back from knee surgery. Imagine a pitcher doing that today.

There was a cover story about his return in *Sports Illustrated*. This was big news. He ended up losing his next start as well but then looked to be back in top form like in 1976, winning six straight games in June. He pitched complete games in seven of the eight starts. In July, in a game versus the Orioles, he felt his arm go dead. He gave up six runs.

His pitching would never be the same. Fidrych pitched twice more that year but didn't get through the first inning on July 12th, which was his final start for the season.

A career that had started out so promising in 1976 had burned out quickly.

His first start for Detroit had come the previous year, on May 15th 1976 against the Indians. The only reason he was starting was because the scheduled pitcher had the flu. He pitched a complete game 2-1 win. He gave up only two hits.

In his third and fourth games he won both games in eleven innings, going the distance in both. He ended up going 19-9 on the season.

He was named American League Rookie of The Year. He led the league in complete games with 24. He finished in the top five in many other statistical categories, too.

After pitching only 11 games in 1977, he attempted a comeback in '78. He pitched three games and went 2-0. In 1979 he only pitched four games and went 0-3. 1980, his last year in Detroit, he pitched in nine games and went 2-3.

Fidrych was released after the 1981 season and signed on with the Boston Red Sox with a minor league deal. He was finally diagnosed with a torn rotator cuff, which had never healed and hindered his pitching. He had the surgery but it was too late.

He was found dead on April 13th 2009 at his farm. His clothes had become entangled in his ten-wheel dump truck. He was 54 years old.

Detroit Tigers fans still talk fondly of the crazy guy with the curls talking to the ball between pitches.

My dad often wonders what could've been if he hadn't been injured in 1977 and had his rotator cuff injury fixed early.

For seven-year-old me, The Bird gave me a memory I still cherish. A trip with my family to see a baseball game I will never forget.

Chapter 22: June 9 - 13. Away v. Biloxi Shuckers

June 9th

The Jumbo Shrimp are now 25-36 after a 6-2 loss to the Shuckers. They're winless against the Shuckers this season and have lost five of their last six games.

Omar Bencomo took the loss and is now 4-4. He went five innings and allowed five runs.

Hunter Adkins came in and had a scoreless inning, followed by a scoreless inning from Esmerling De La Rosa.

Taylor Ard hit a home run in the fourth inning.

I see big roster moves coming soon for the team. The pitching and hitting are both faltering at the same time lately.

Something's gotta give. Right?

June 10th

A 5-2 win by the Jumbo Shrimp has restored some of my faith in the team… if they can build on it. Starter Joe Gunkel got his first Southern League win with a strong seven inning performance. He gave up one unearned run on five hits. He struck out three and retired the last nine batters he faced. Daniel Schlereth took care of the Shuckers in the eighth in order. Andy Beltre got the final three outs.

It's the first win against the Shuckers all season.

June 11th

A second win against the Shuckers, this time in big fashion. 13-1.

Starter Matt Tomshaw (now 6-3) went seven innings, only allowing a run with three walks and three strikeouts.

In the third inning the Shuckers gave up four consecutive walks and the Jumbo Shrimp took a 5-1 lead.

Shortstop Chris Diaz got his first hit as a Jumbo Shrimp with a two-run single. They scored six runs in the inning.

The hitting wasn't over as they tacked on four runs in the fourth inning.

Jacksonville had fourteen hits. Left fielder Jeremias Pineda went 3-for-3. Austin Nola, Chris Diaz and Alex Yarbrough each collected two hits. In addition, Nola and Diaz both knocked in four runs apiece. They also had a season-high eleven walks.

Tayron Guerrero had a perfect eight and Tyler Higgins finished it off with a perfect ninth.

Speaking of Higgins, I got to talk to the pitcher during the season as well.

Who were some of your heroes growing up?

"I really liked the Tigers. I'm from Michigan. I liked watching Derek Jeter with the Yankees because he's from Michigan as well. He was a big name you grew up hearing about. Jeremy Bonderman was a big Tigers guy. I liked Brandon Inge, who played third base for the Tigers for a long time."

How does Double-A compare to Single-A?

"The game's a lot faster. The lineups are a lot better. You're playing in a lot bigger cities. The travel is a little longer. The first day in a new city you're a lot more tired. I look at it this way: the best four hitters from every team move up. You get into a team where the best four hitters from last year are batting at the back of the order and the new guys are filling in another four spots at the top of the order. The team is getting better every year. As a pitcher I have to make adjustments to that."

Is it hard as a pitcher to adjust with so much movement in the minors?

"It's tough. You see certain guys multiple times. You might face a guy in Low A and then in High A and then here. They're also making adjustments. As everyone progresses I'm not the same pitcher and they're not the same hitter. The higher up you get the more people are weeded out. The players who aren't making the adjustments to better themselves you won't see again."

In corresponding moves, righty Joe Gunkel was promoted to New Orleans and lefty Greg Nappo was sent down.

June 12th

The Jumbo Shrimp lost 3-0. I've never played baseball (or any sports) professionally so I might be completely missing the point, but I wonder how you can score thirteen runs one night and then get shutout the next. I see it all the time. Is it mental? Are you wiped from hitting so much the night before or do you get too comfortable? Someday I need to ask a player that very question.

Righty Hunter Adkins took the loss, giving up two runs on six hits in four innings of work. Greg Nappo took over, pitching two innings. He had two hits and a run against. Clayton Mortensen fared better, turning in two perfect innings.

Jeremias Pineda and Austin Nola got the only hits for the Jumbo Shrimp.

June 13th

Another loss to end this series, 5-2. Biloxi lefty reliever Nick Ramirez not only got the win with three scoreless innings but also hit a grand slam in the sixth off of pitcher Junichi Tazawa, on rehab assignment from the Miami Marlins. In ⅔ of an inning Tazawa allowed those four runs and gave up five hits. He struck out two.

Jacksonville has yet to win a road series as the first half of the season is coming to a close. They're also winless in five tries in rubber matches on the road, meaning the last and deciding game when a series is tied.

Chapter 23: June 14 - 18. Home vs. Pensacola Blue Wahoos And June 20 - North vs. South All-Star Game

June 14th

No game. Lots of rain. Hurricane Cindy was making her presence known. I love 99% of living in Florida. A hurricane (and no good pizza - trust me) is the 1% I dislike.

Pitcher Tyler Higgins was placed on the 7-Day DL and pitcher Joe Gunkel was sent down from New Orleans.

June 15th

A rain-shortened six inning game and a 1-0 loss. The second game of the doubleheader was cancelled and will (hopefully) be made up tomorrow. This weather is playing havoc with the end of the first-half schedule.

Starter Joe Gunkel took a heartbreaking loss, pitching five innings and scattering three hits and three walks with a strikeout. The lone run came when he walked a batter, who went to second on a groundout. A two-out single drove him in.

Rehabbing pitcher Junichi Tazawa struck out the only batter he faced before the weather got too bad to continue the game. The game at this point was official.

After a delay, in which I ate another jumbo hot dog and had another Diet Coke in a souvenir cup, the game was officially over and the second game cancelled.

With the win Pensacola's magic number to clinch the first half was down to one.

Lefty Daniel Schlereth was promoted to New Orleans and Lefty Chris O'Grady swapped places with him.

June 16th

Let's (try to) play two. Two seven inning games.

In the first game the Blue Wahoos won, 9-3, and clinched the first half.

Marlins third baseman Martin Prado and shortstop Adeiny Hechavarria were both on rehab assignment and both had two at-bats in the game. Prado got a hit. My wife had me look up their salaries and wasn't impressed with either, especially making so much more than any Jumbo Shrimp player. She's way more cut-and-dry than I am.

Jacksonville won the second game, 1-0.

Mike Kickham went five innings for his fourth win of the season.

June 17th

Another game postponed due to rain. Last time I checked this was the Sunshine State. Maybe two games tomorrow to close out the first half of the season?

More from my conversation with relief pitcher Tyler Higgins.

Raudel Lazo was one of our players we were boosters for but then he was released. Is it weird for you to have someone as a teammate one day and the next he's been cut?

"It's normal. I've been in this league for four years. Been a Marlin for seven. It's completely normal for me. You can see when stuff is coming ahead of times in some cases. The younger guys get shocked. They get nerved up about it. After awhile it just becomes normal. It's part of the business. It sucks. None of it is fun."

Does it change your pitching and approach when you know you have some great defensive players behind you?

"Sometimes. I try not to think about it like that. It might not change my approach but after something happens and someone makes a great play behind you you're thankful."

What's your normal game day routine?

"Every day I might have a chance to get in there. I do little things each day to get ready. Nothing similar each day."

Do you ever get an idea what days you'll pitch based on the last game or two?

"Towards the end of the season you get a feel for it. The starters start going longer. Six or seven innings, which mean the bullpen innings are getting shorter. We're not getting as much use. It becomes a revolving door. Every three or four days you might be called on to pitch an inning. Maybe two. You just wait for your turn."

Sitting in the bullpen, especially out in the open like at home, how do you pass the time?

"There are a lot of fans who've been coming out for the past three or four years. Fans I know personally. They'll sit near us every home game. You get those who come every Thursday. We might talk for a few seconds with the fans but we're paying attention to the game. I take a chart every game of the other team's hitters and what they did throughout the entire game."

Do you go out there relaxed on the field or trying to do your absolute best to get moved up?

"There are guys who think about it. There are some players who are really streaky. Others are very consistent. The players who are consistent stay where they are and continue to do their thing no matter what happens. They're set in their routine and they're the same guy every time. The guys who are too worried about where their cleats are or aren't usually are the guys who streak high and low."

The giveaway for the game was a Jumbo Shrimp neck pillow. Shaped like a shrimp. We got in early thanks to being season ticket holders and they were very cool. They won the month's giveaway promotion for all of Minor League baseball.

A couple of nights later, while watching TV, I said my neck hurt. My wife took out the neck pillows and we sat next to each other on the couch and used them.

We looked goofy but they're really comfortable.

I might or might not use one during the day to nap when she's at work.

June 18th

Great way to end the first half. The Jumbo Shrimp took both games, 3-2 and 1-0, in seven innings apiece.

5,138 fans got to see a great Sunday of baseball.

Starter Omar Bencomo went three innings and gave up a solo homer in the first. Junichi Tazawa, still on rehab, pitched a perfect inning and struck out two. Severino Gonzalez got the win with 2 ⅓ innings, giving up one run on three hits with three strikeouts. Clayton Mortensen pitched the last ⅔ inning to get the save.

Rehabbing Prado and Hechavarria each went 1-for-3. Cam Maron hit his second home run of the season.

In game two, starter Chris Mazza scattered five hits and a walk, striking out three.

Andy Beltre pitched the last inning to get the win. He gave up three hits and struck out two.

The only scoring came in the bottom of the seventh. Catcher Austin Nola singles. Brian Anderson was hit by a pitch. John Norwood struck out but then Taylor Ard was walked. With the bases loaded and one out, Alex Glenn hit the first pitch he saw down the right-field line, scoring Austin Nola with the winning run.

It was a great way to end the first half and hopefully a preview of what the second half of the season will look like.

The Jumbo Shrimp ended up 30-40, ten games under .500. The Blue Wahoos ended with a 40-30 record and a spot in the playoffs at the end of the year.

Lefty Chris O'Grady was promoted to New Orleans. Pitchers Hunter Adkins and Greg Nappo were released.

I'm guessing there will be some roster changes as we get into the second half of the season.

June 20th All-Star Game

Tropical Storm Cindy was the MVP this year, cancelling the Southern League All-Star Game in Pensacola. It would've been the first time hosting the event for the Blue Wahoos Stadium.

It was the first Southern League All-Star Game rainout in thirty-seven years.

The last rainout? It was in 1980 in Jacksonville.

Next year the Birmingham Barons will host. I'm already looking at the calendar to see if we'll head that way in 2018 to see the game.

Pitcher Trevor Richards was promoted from Jupiter and third baseman Matt Juengel was sent down from New Orleans.

Chapter 24: Brooks Robinson

In 1977 my dad also piled us into the car and we headed for another baseball road trip, this time to see Brooks Robinson of the Baltimore Orioles play in his last game.

He'd been playing sporadically by late July of '77 and only appeared in two games in August, both as a pinch-hitter. Rick Dempsey was coming off of the disabled list and Brooks decided it was time to retire from the game.

"We just decided to go," my dad said. *"I'm a diehard Tigers fan but I respected other players. Robinson was one of them. He was probably my favorite non-Tigers player. I hated any Yankees players. I didn't care about Mantle or any of them."*

I can definitely relate, as being a Red Sox fan I still appreciated everything Cal Ripken Jr. did on the field. He was a player I loved to watch.

Plus, I hated the Yankees as much as my dad did, too.

"It was the old Memorial Stadium. We got seats right behind the dugout on the first base side. One row back. Just by walking up to the ticket window. It was brutally hot and everyone was on the other side

of the field. We were almost the only people sitting on that side of the stadium."

Dad had a broken foot with a cast on it. My brother and I had our gloves on and there was no one around us. If a ball was hit near us we'd get it. One did come close but we didn't get it. As the game progressed and the sun moved more people filled in around us but the regulars knew where to sit and stay out of the sun. Back then they didn't change the scheduling of games, so it was a 1pm game and they weren't going to move it to later. Today, if it was his last game, they'd move it to 8pm and have it on TV on ESPN or MLB Network.

"I bet there weren't three thousand people in the stands, which is a shame. By the time the game was into the fifth or sixth inning there might've been fifteen thousand there. It was a work day. People were still at work," dad said.

I don't remember much about the game at all. In 1977 I was seven, so the fun was the trip to get to Baltimore from New Jersey, which seemed like it took forever.

Years later, when I was in high school and then in my twenties, I'd take the drive to Baltimore to see the Red Sox in town and get some delicious crab cakes as well. It didn't seem nearly as long.

Brooks Robinson was inducted into the Baseball Hall of Fame in 1983 on the first ballot. It was a given after the years he'd played the game and the high level he'd done it at.

He was signed by the Baltimore Orioles as an amateur free agent in 1955. He played his entire career with the team.

In 1964 he won the American League MVP Award. In 1966 he was the All-Star Game MVP. He was also the World Series MVP in 1970.

In his illustrious career Brooks was on the All-Star team fifteen consecutive years. He played in four World Series. He dominated in so many offensive and defensive categories.

His twenty-three seasons with one team set a major league record until Carl Yastrzemski broke it. Only Yaz, Hank Aaron and Stan Musial played more games for one franchise.

While the exact games and plays might be fuzzy after forty years and hundreds (perhaps thousands) of games in-between, there's one thing I'm certain about: Brooks Robinson was a very special player to my dad.

It is yet another cherished baseball memory we share as a family.

Chapter 25: June 22 - 26. Away Vs. Jackson Generals

June 22nd

A loss to begin the second half of the season, 5-2.

Starter Joe Gunkel took the loss (he's now 1-4) with four earned runs on eight hits in six innings.

The Jumbo Shrimp got on the board in the seventh with RBI singles from Alex Yarbrough and Austin Nola.

After an hour rain delay in the middle of the seventh inning the game resumed. Except for a solo home run from the Generals off of reliever Esmerling De La Rosa, the game coasted until the end.

There were a few roster moves, as pitcher Omar Bencomo was put on the 7-Day DL, pitcher Tyler Higgins was activated from the DL, pitcher Jeff Kinley was promoted from Jupiter, and pitcher Daniel Schlereth came back from New Orleans.

June 23rd

The Jumbo Shrimp got the 9-4 victory, with starter Trevor Richards making his debut and earning the win. He pitched 5 ⅓ innings, allowing three runs on seven hits. He had three walks and three strikeouts.

Right fielder John Norwood went 3-for-6 with his tenth home run of the season. Norwood and third baseman Brian Anderson are now tied with ten for the team and it will be interesting to see how many each player will get before they're promoted to Triple-A, which is inevitable to me.

June 24th

It was a 3-1 loss as the Jumbo Shrimp keep bouncing back and forth from loss to win to loss in the beginning of the second half.

Starter Mike Kickham got the loss, his first since late April. He's now 4-4. He gave up three runs on seven hits and struck out five in six innings. Tyler Higgins and Tayron Guerrero both pitched a scoreless inning in relief.

I guess Brian Anderson didn't want to share the team home run lead with John Norwood because he smashed his eleventh in the first inning.

June 25th

Jacksonville lost, 1-0 in a pitching duel between the two teams. It was decided on a wild pitch by Jeff Kinley, making his Jumbo Shrimp debut, in the seventh inning, which allowed the Generals to score from third.

Chris Mazza had started and worked six scoreless innings with only three hits against him. He walked two and struck out two. He hasn't allowed a run in his last 21 innings.

The Jumbo Shrimp bats have been anemic. They haven't scored in 17 innings. They're 0-8 in road series so far this year, too.

Something's gotta give. I might be crazy, but they just need a streak to get back in this. They don't look like they're having fun out there. Most guys are scuffling, trying to make the big play or get the big at-bat to turn the season around.

June 26th

The Jumbo Shrimp got a win, 2-1, behind Matt Tomshaw (7-4) going six innings and only giving up a run. Daniel Schlereth got the final two outs to earn his second save.

I have to point out something about Daniel. He's a pitcher who's had a taste of the Majors. He was drafted by the Arizona Diamondbacks, 26th pick, in the 2008 MLB Draft. He made his debut in relief against the Atlanta Braves the following year on May 29th 2009. He pitched a perfect inning.

In December he was traded along with pitcher Max Scherzer to the Detroit Tigers. He was called up to the Tigers on July 2nd 2010. On August 15th 2011 he gave up Jim Thome's 600th home run.

He bounced around organizations for the next few years, playing in Triple-A. In April of this year, just as the season started, he signed with the Marlins and landed in Jacksonville.

In his early thirties, Daniel is most likely a guy who's a long-shot to make it back to the Majors. He's a veteran on this young Jumbo Shrimp team and as I watch him throughout the season I can't help but think he has a pitching coach term in his future. He's usually the pitcher getting signs from Storm Davis and getting pitchers warmed up. He runs back and forth between the bullpen and dugout several times each game.

The guy seems like someone you'd want on your team, especially if you were a young pitcher. His knowledge can only help.

And he comes from an athletic family. His father played in the NFL for twelve seasons with the Washington Redskins and Denver Broncos and started in three Super Bowls at guard. He's currently an ESPN analyst and has a recurring role on HBO's *Ballers* with The Rock.

It was our pleasure helping Daniel out with snacks and drinks this season. Finding out he was married and has two daughters and he's so far away from home, still living his dream, is inspiring.

Back to the game.

John Norwood drove in both runs with two RBI singles.

Catcher Chris Hoo was sent down to Jupiter and left fielder Kyle Barrett came up from Jupiter.

Chapter 26: June 28 - July 3. Home vs. Mobile BayBears

June 28th

The Miami Marlins traded shortstop Adeiny Hechavarria, who'd been on rehab with the Jumbo Shrimp not too long ago, to the Tampa Bay Rays in exchange for pitcher Ethan Clark and center fielder Braxton Lee.

Braxton Lee, who I'd been following all year when the Jumbo Shrimp played the Biscuits. When he was added to the Jumbo Shrimp roster I was quite excited. My wife thought I was too excited.

I think she started to understand when she saw Braxton on our side. He went 2-for-4 and started the game hitting leadoff and getting an infield single.

The other newcomer to the team, right fielder Kyle Barrett, went 3-for-4 batting second in the lineup. Add in a John Norwood home run, his eleventh, and a 4-2 win for the team and I'd say as a fan it was a great night of baseball. I think the 2,906 fans in attendance agreed.

Joe Gunkel got the win giving up two runs on four hits in seven innings. At one point he retired fifteen of sixteen batters he faced.

Severino Gonzalez got the last two outs of the ninth inning to record his first save of the season.

Unfortunately, because of the addition of Braxton Lee to the team, center fielder Alex Glenn, who was hitting .179, was released. *"I was truly devastated,"* my wife said. *"He always had a smile on his face. He was one of my favorite players. It was so sad that I wouldn't be able to see him play anymore."*

Left fielder Austin Dean, out most of the season, was sent to the Gulf Coast Marlins on a rehab assignment. It would be great to have him back before the end of the season.

June 29th

The weather was the winner tonight, halting the game at the top of the fifth inning. The suspended game will be finished tomorrow night, followed by a seven inning game.

Before the rain shut it down, Starter Trevor Richards had a great game, not allowing a hit until the fourth inning. During a close play at the plate thanks to a great throw from left fielder Jeremias Pineda to catcher Austin Nola, it looked like the runner was out.

Manager Randy Ready disagreed with the call and the home plate umpire and was ejected.

Braxton Lee had another leadoff single to start the game.

Once the top of the fifth was in the books they called the game. This was the first suspended game for either team.

I guess we'll get some bonus baseball tomorrow night.

Third Baseman David Vidal was assigned to the team along with catcher Rodrigo Vigil.

June 30th

Braxton Lee is something else. He added three more hits to this game (he had one yesterday in the beginning of it, which sounds odd) and the Jumbo Shrimp got a 6-3 win out of it. And it didn't come easy.

There was a three hour rain delay before the bottom of the fifth could begin. 5,284 fans stuck around for the end of this game and a seven inning second one and then got treated to fireworks on a rainy Friday night.

Brian Anderson hit his twelfth home run of the season and Tyler Higgins went two innings, only giving up a run, to get the victory.

In game two Jacksonville won again, this time 2-1. Starter Mike Kickham (now 5-4) went all seven innings for the win. He gave up one run on four hits and looked impressive again.

First baseman Taylor Ard hit his seventh homer of the season.

Even with the horrible weather, the Jumbo Shrimp seem like they're beginning to gel on the field. More smiles for the players. The fans can tell something special might be happening.

My fingers are crossed.

Catcher Austin Nola was promoted to New Orleans. Third baseman Rehiner Cordova went on the 7-Day DL. Second baseman David Vidal came back from New Orleans. Catcher Rodrigo Vigil promoted from Jupiter.

July 1st

MLB legend Vince Coleman, a Raines High School star, threw out the first pitch. As season ticket holders we were allowed to get in early and get the night's giveaway, a Vince Coleman bobblehead. Later on I'd give the second one to my buddy Pat Marz, who shares my birthday and love of baseball. He's a Cardinals fan so I hope he liked it.

During a rain delay Clayton, our account manager, let us go into one of the empty skyboxes in the stadium to get out of the brutal heat of Florida. I began pestering my wife about how much we needed our own box. Think of the possibilities. We could invite twenty of our closest friends to each game. Air conditioned room. Seats outside with a great view of the field.

While she loved sitting in such comfort and watching the game once it started back up, I think I need to work on her a bit more.

Someday I'll get it and you're all invited. All I ask is that you bring me up a jumbo hot dog (plain) and a Diet Coke in a Jumbo Shrimp souvenir cup. Fair?

When play resumed the Jumbo Shrimp got their fifth straight win, 6-4, in front of 4,438 fans. You can feel the electricity and it wasn't just because we were in the skybox, either.

You can see it on the player's faces. They believe they can win any game they play. What was lacking in the first half was them being loose and enjoying the game.

They played fundamental baseball in this one, knocking in each run with precision. No giant dramatic home runs tonight. Just sound hitting and running.

Andy Beltre got the win with two perfect innings, breezing through the fourth and fifth. He's now 3-0 on the year. Severino Gonzalez picked up his second save.

Catcher Rodrigo Vigil is on a tear so far in his brief tenure with the Jumbo Shrimp. Today he went 3-for-4 with an RBI and he's gone 5-for-6 so far.

I'll take a rain delay every game if I knew they'd end up winning that game.

Maybe try to sneak into a skybox again to wait out the delay, though.

July 2nd

My wife couldn't come to the game. Instead, I got to hang out with The Terror Twins all day and go to a Sunday afternoon game with them.

The Terror Twins are my nephews, Austin and Aiden. They're, like ten and eleven… something like that. I obviously don't pay attention unless it has to do with baseball. They enjoy sports but more importantly they were going to run and get my food and drink so I could watch the game.

I miss my own kids when they were that little.

Starter Matt Tomshaw (8-4) pitched another great game, going seven innings while giving up only two runs. Clayton Mortensen pitched the ninth inning for his third save.

Catcher Cam Maron hit his third home run of the season.

Center fielder Braxton Lee went 2-for-4 and hit his third homer of the season, too. It was his first as a Jumbo Shrimp. He's leading the Southern League with a .337 batting average, 95 hits and 52 runs. This guy is special.

July 3rd

The six game winning streak has ended, but the Jumbo Shrimp are still riding tall at the top of the South Division.

The crowd was monstrous: 11,398, the biggest crowd in nine years. They came to see great baseball and great fireworks to cap off the night.

A personal highlight for me was seeing my wife win the GM's Money, a nightly contest where you text your seat to the GM, Harold Craw, and he gives one lucky fan a crisp hundred dollar bill. She got to be on the big screen and seen by the biggest crowd, too.

Afterwards her cousin texted to let her know she was at the game and saw her, which was nice.

Joe Gunkel had his worst start of the season, going 2 ⅔ innings. He gave up eight runs on eight hits. Four relievers came in and shut down the BayBears but it was too late.

A positive for the Jumbo Shrimp was left fielder Austin Dean making his return to the team after being out since the first week of the season. He started off nicely, going 2-for-3.

Third Baseman Brian Anderson hit his thirteenth home run of the season, too.

To make room for Austin Dean the Jumbo Shrimp released Jeremias Pineda and placed pitcher Tayron Guerrero on the temporarily inactive list.

Chapter 27: Pine Tar Game

There are certain sporting events that people swear they were at. I watched a documentary about great football games and one of the games was played in front of 30,000 people. The joke from the players years later was that they met 130,000 people who mention they were at the game.

I've met a few people who will tell me they were at the infamous Pine Tar Game. When I tell them I was also there and begin to talk about it, they usually smile and change the subject because they might've seen it on TV in 1983 or (more than likely) they've seen the iconic clip of George Brett rushing from the dugout when the ump calls him out.

I was there.

Every year my Uncle Armand would take me, my brother and my cousin Armand (I think I already mentioned all first males on the Rosamilia side were named Armand. Armando, actually, but we go by Armand) to a Yankees game. It didn't matter who they played. The three of them were Yankees fans. I was the weird kid.

Looking back, I'm guessing Uncle Armand took me to see the Red Sox at least once. I guess it depended on when he could take off from work and when he could get tickets.

It was July 24th, 1983. A normal Sunday. I was 13. Yankees vs. Royals. 33,944 in actual attendance.

I don't remember much about the game up until the ninth. At that point it was just another Yankees game and I know I was secretly rooting against them. I couldn't actually cheer when the other team scored except inside. I also couldn't wear any Red Sox stuff to the game, either. That was a big no-no.

Top of the ninth. Yankees are winning, 4-3. Not that shocking to me, since I don't remember ever seeing a Yankees-Red Sox game in person when the Yankees lost. I'm a jinx.

As we'd say in Jersey, I'm what is known as a *mush.* Bad luck.

George Brett steps to the plate with two outs. We were sitting in left field down the third base line. The upper deck was above us and I can still picture the overhang blocking the view when Brett hit the ball and it went sailing into right.

The crowd moaned and yelled around us and my uncle was beside himself.

Because our seats weren't the best and far away, Uncle Armand had brought his binoculars with him.

When it was obvious there was something going on after the home run, he passed them to us and we took turns watching and trying to figure out what had happened.

I'm not sure if it was my brother or cousin who started yelling Brett was out. I could see him charge from the dugout and his coach and teammates held him back.

If you're even a casual baseball fan you already know what happened: Yankees manager Billy Martin had been tipped by one of his players about the excessive use of pine tar on Brett's bat. The rule was put in place not because it gave the batter an unfair advantage (like, say, Albert Belle corking his bat in the 1990's) but because the pine tar would ruin a ball if it hit it and they were ruining too many balls. It had to do with cost and nothing more.

But it was still a rule.

Billy Martin didn't say a word about the bat until Brett had done damage against the Yankees. He ran out and explained to the umpiring crew the bat was illegal.

I can still remember the ump placing the bat next to home plate and then calling George Brett out. The home run didn't count. Three outs. Game over.

Obviously the pro-Yankees crowd went wild.

I was, once again, a *mush*. Would I ever see the Yankees lose in person?

When we walked to my Uncle Armand's car he smiled and I remember him telling us to never lose the ticket stub because this was an important game.

I went home and after excitedly explaining the game to my parents, who'd watched it on TV and saw it as well, I put the ticket stub away in my drawer for safekeeping.

Yes, I still have it in a box somewhere. I haven't seen it in years but I know it is still in my possession.

The Royals protested the game. It was upheld and the game had to be played from the point of the home run. On August 18th it officially ended. I remember watching that game on TV, where the

Yankees tossed to first, second and third to say Brett didn't touch all the bases. It was a last-ditch attempt and didn't work.

The Royals lost and George Brett became one of the greatest non-Red Sox players I've ever watched.

During a visit to the Baseball Hall of Fame I saw the bat on display.

I'm sure when I was excitedly telling whoever I was with I was at the game the other visitors to the Hall in earshot must've laughed, thinking I was one of the hundreds of thousands who swore I was there.

But I was.

Chapter 28: July 4 - 8. Away vs. Montgomery Biscuits

July 4th

The Jumbo Shrimp defeated the Biscuits 10-1 on Independence Day in front of 7,082 fans. They're now 8-4 in the second half.

Starter Trevor Richards got his second win with six strong innings, allowing a run on four hits. He struck out six. Andy Beltre pitched two perfect innings in relief and Daniel Schlereth pitched the ninth to finish it up.

Brian Anderson has been on fire lately. He hit his fourteenth home run of the season. He's my daughter's favorite player and I keep teasing her she needs to stare at him as much as possible while she can because he'll be promoted soon. For some reason she doesn't think I'm funny.

Former Biscuit Braxton Lee went 1-for-3 with an RBI single. John Norwood was back, going 3-for-5 and scoring twice. He'd been out of the lineup since he came out of Sunday's game.

Righty Scott Copeland was sent down from New Orleans.

July 5th

Starter Mike Kickham went five innings and gave up four runs on eight hits, taking the loss in a 5-3 game.

Right fielder John Norwood hit his twelfth home run of the season. He went 2-for-3 and David Vidal went 2-for-4. The only other hit for the Jumbo Shrimp was a double by catcher Cam Maron, driving in the second run for the team.

Lefty Dillon Peters was sent to Gulf Coast Marlins on a rehab assignment.

July 6th

The Jumbo Shrimp lost, 11-5, in the third game of this series. It's tough as a fan to not be at the game, even though Roger Hoover calls a phenomenal game and makes you feel like you're there. My problem is I like to see the team on the field. Between innings. Get a sense of how they're managing with losses and enjoying wins.

Righty starter Chris Mazza took the loss. He's now 1-5 on the season. He allowed four runs on eight hits, walking two and striking out a pair. He only lasted four innings before Jeff Kinley came in, but he was ineffective as well. In 1 ⅔ innings he gave up three runs on only one hit but three walks. Severino Gonzalez came in and pitched 1 ⅓ inning but he gave up two runs on three hits. Finally, Andy Beltre pitched the final inning. He gave up the final two runs on three hits and a walk. It was not a good night for Jumbo Shrimp pitching.

On the hitting side, David Vidal had a hit, extending his hitting streak to seven games. Braxton Lee and John Norwood both had two hits.

July 7th

Another rainout. I'm hoping it gives the team a chance to regroup, take a deep breath and come out fighting tomorrow.

Pitcher Chris Mazza was sent down to Jupiter. As much as I like seeing him pitch, he's been ineffective for too many innings at a time. Maybe he'll recover some of the things that make him impressive for short stretches. Pitcher Eric Alonzo moved up to take his spot.

July 8th

It was a doubleheader loss for the Jumbo Shrimp as the Biscuits won 6-4 and 3-0. They've now lost four straight and have still not won a road series this year.

Starter Matt Tomshaw went five innings, allowing six runs on eight hits for the loss. Tyler Higgins pitched the sixth inning, giving up two hits and no runs.

First baseman Taylor Ard hit his eighth home run of the season.

In the second game starter Joe Gunkel took the loss. He went five innings, allowing three runs on four hits. He struck out six. Daniel Schlereth pitched a perfect inning for the Jumbo Shrimp.

The Jacksonville bats were silenced, with only two hits.

Biscuits starting pitcher Hunter Adkins went four innings, giving up two hits and two walks while striking out two. He played for the Jumbo Shrimp the first half of the season before being cut.

Third baseman Rehiner Cordova was activated from the disabled list. Pitcher Scott Copeland was promoted back to New Orleans. Pitcher Chris Mazza came back from Jupiter and the team placed third baseman Brian Anderson on the temporarily inactive list… but for a good reason. He'd be one of the Jumbo Shrimp players going to the Futures Game.

Chapter 29: July 9 - 12. Home vs. Biloxi Shuckers

July 9th

3,818 fans were treated to a pitching duel on a Sunday afternoon, and it was Christmas in July, too.

Starter Trevor Richards went seven innings, scattering three hits and a walk while striking out ten. Relievers Clayton Mortensen and Daniel Schlereth each pitched a scoreless inning. In extra innings, Severino Gonzalez pitched the tenth and eleventh, striking out two and only giving up a hit to get the win, 1-0.

The winning run for the Jumbo Shrimp came with two out in the bottom of the eleventh. With Rehiner Cordova on third base and John Norwood at the plate and with two strikes, a wild pitch got past the catcher and allowed Cordova to run home and score.

The win was not only dramatic but it put Jacksonville in first place.

David Vidal went 1-for-4 as the Jumbo Shrimp third baseman, which was only important because the normal third baseman, Brian Anderson, was down in

Miami playing in the Futures Game as part of the MLB All-Star Game excitement.

Against the best prospects in baseball, Anderson went 2-for-4 with a double and a run scored for Team USA, who won 7-6. He was in the lineup as designated hitter before going to third base to close out the game.

Equally exciting was having pitcher Tayron Guerrero pitching for Team World. He faced two batters in the eighth inning, getting outfielder Lewis Brinson to fly out and outfielder Corey Ray to groundout.

I can only imagine how exciting it was for both players, hoping someday they'd be on that field playing for the Miami Marlins.

July 10th

I didn't go to the game tonight. A rare missed Jumbo Shrimp game but my wife had tickets to see the Jacksonville Sharks in the inaugural National Arena League Championship game, which they won 27-21.

We had fun and it was an exciting game but when we left the arena right across the street from the Baseball Grounds I felt like I'd been unfaithful to the Jumbo Shrimp.

I guess I was a *mush*, because the Jumbo Shrimp lost 8-4 in front of a small crowd of 1,549 on a Monday night.

It was like a home run derby (which was happening in Miami tonight for the MLB Home Run

Derby) as Austin Dean hit his second and John Norwood hit his thirteenth.

But the Shuckers countered with right fielder Michael Choice, who hit three home runs tonight. Even their pitcher, Aaron Wilkerson, hit a homer tonight.

Righty Eric Alonzo made his Jumbo Shrimp debut after starter Mike Kickham was knocked out of the game. Alonzo went 2 ⅓ innings, giving up a run.

July 11th

I hope Taylor Ard wasn't too comfortable riding the bench until the ninth inning. With one out in the top of the ninth, the Jumbo Shrimp did a double-switch so pitcher Clayton Mortensen could pitch in a tied game. Mortensen got the two outs to preserve the tie.

Ard then lead off with a double in the bottom of the ninth. Center fielder Braxton Lee was intentionally walked. He'd already gone 3-for-4 today. I guess they didn't want him to beat them. Then third baseman Brian Anderson was walked. Not intentional. It loaded the bases.

John Norwood is at bat. He doesn't have the chance to be the hero with his bat because a wild pitch scores Taylor Ard with the winning run.

Miami Marlins infielder Miguel Rojas, on a rehab assignment, played shortstop and all nine innings in the 4-3 victory.

Brian Anderson, after his successful Futures Game, was back in the lineup and on the roster. To make room the Jumbo Shrimp released third baseman Rehiner Cordova. Pitcher Tayron Guerrero was also back from the Futures Game. With this move, pitcher Eric Alonzo was shipped back to Jupiter.

July 12th

5,819 fans took in a Wednesday afternoon game and saw another win, 3-2.

John Norwood smacked his third walk-off homer of the season in the bottom of the tenth inning. It was his fourteenth home run of the season and tied him for the team lead with Brian Anderson. The pair is also third in home runs in the Southern League.

Righty Omar Bencomo pitched five scoreless innings with three hits and four strikeouts. He also picked off two base runners on first base.

With a 1-0 lead in the eighth, Severino Gonzalez gave up a two-run homer to Biloxi.

In the bottom of the inning rehabbing Miguel Rojas had a leadoff single. John Norwood, future hero of the game, singled to put runners at the corners. Cam Maron hit a sacrifice fly to tie it up.

Mortensen pitched a scoreless top of the tenth. Manager Randy Ready was thrown out of the game for arguing a Cam Maron throwing error. The kids in attendance, and there were a lot of them, cheered when he walked back to the dugout, shaking his head.

Then the Norwood drama that seems to get better each time he does it.

I did something I don't normally do during a game: I left my seat. I know… crazy.

Between the sun beating down on my bald head, even with my Jumbo Shrimp hat on and drinking a Diet Coke (in a souvenir cup, of course) I was getting thirsty about halfway through the game. My wife wasn't with me so I had to fend for myself like an animal. Maybe I'm being a bit dramatic.

Clayton Edwards, our account rep, always came over at some point during a game to say hi to us. I stood in the shade with Clayton and chatted for awhile.

I told him I was going to get lemonade. I was in the mood. Warm day. Lots of sun. It just sounded right. Clayton told me he wanted to introduce me to the owner of the stand, Lemonball Lemonade, Brad Yurkovich. I got a chance to talk to him for the book, too.

How did Lemonball Lemonade begin?

"It started four years ago but we have been doing lemonade for six. We started out as The Main Squeeze Lemonade, which we still use in Akron, Ohio. I always wanted to own my own business but all my ideas were very expensive and I didn't have the money. Until one day a friend said he was opening a hotdog stand and I said if you do that I will do lemonade because they go well together. Thinking about it I realized in our area no one has ever branded a lemonade stand before so I pitched the idea to my wife and we used our tax return to start Main Squeeze. How I got to LemonBall Lemonade is that I played high school and some college baseball and it's just been in my blood. I thought: what's better than baseball and lemonade? With us growing out of state I had to trademark the name and Main

Squeeze wasn't protectable so we decided to rebrand our baseball stadium stands to LemonBall Lemonade after an image I found seven years ago that I thought looked cool. Someone literally photoshopped baseball stitches on a lemon and I thought it looked cool and always held on to it. I didn't know that it would play such a pivotal role in naming my company years later," Brad said.

How did you get involved with Ken Babby and the Akron team?

"I knew I wanted to get involved with Minor League Baseball with the lemonade because I believed it hit more of our demographic. More of a friendly family environment. I didn't know anything about Ken or the Akron team before I approached them. One day I just sent an email and introduced myself and what we could offer their fans. Jim Pfander brought us in for a meeting and tasting. They obviously loved it. Four seasons later and it has been awesome."

So you worked with the management in Akron. How did you land a stand in Jacksonville as well?

"When I first heard the rumor that Ken might be buying a new team I immediately wanted to be involved. It didn't matter where, either. I wanted to keep working with Ken. I was working at the stand in Akron when Ken came up and I jokingly said Hey I heard a rumor and if it's true I want in. *He literally said you're in. That was in July. Ken didn't take over the team in Jacksonville until November and I didn't have a deal in place until January, which is very late. But through it all Ken was true to his word. It was scary. I'm not going to lie. Not only going out of state*

but going 13 hours away. No one in the Jacksonville organization knew who I was. I was just a guy from Akron coming down to sell lemonade but they took me in like family. I cannot say enough about the Jacksonville organization. They are truly amazing. When you live in Ohio and you have an excuse to go to Florida anytime you want... it has pretty awesome."

How has business been so far in the Baseball Grounds?

"I love Jacksonville. I didn't know anything about Jacksonville. To me it was a pass through city to get to Orlando and Daytona. The stadium is a little different than the other stadiums as I feel like it's more of a Triple-A team vibe. More of a beer and dog crowd. I know I need to evolve a little differently down here than I do in Ohio. I'm not quite sure what that is yet but we are brewing up something, whether it's updates to our stand or even our servings."

Brad also told me a cool thing I didn't know.

"LemonBall actually has a part of baseball history as they used to play with a Lemon Ball in the mid 19th century. They named it that for its lemon peel look."

To top it all off, Brad even bought me lemonade. It hit the spot.

Baseball in the sun on a hot summer day sipping lemonade… it doesn't get any better than this.

Chapter 30: October 20th 1993 - Philadelphia Phillies vs. Toronto Blue Jays (World Series Game 4)

I was working in the mailroom for a roofing supply company and one of the big bosses was a huge Phillies fan. His teenage son was hanging around the office waiting to go to the game but there was a big chance of rain.

About two hours before game time the boss popped into the mailroom, knowing I was a big baseball fan. He asked if I wanted the two tickets. Of course I grabbed them.

I felt awful when I saw his son, on the verge of tears, leaving the office with his dad.

I'm sure as soon as he got home he watched the game and was really mad at his father for weeks afterwards.

Not completely sure the game was going to be played before heavy rains came, I decided to take the chance and go. I just needed someone to give the second ticket to.

The only person to call was my dad to see if he wanted to go. Truth be told, I was also broke and knew if I took anyone else I wouldn't have money for parking or a hot dog.

I do know that even if I had money for a hot dog I would've asked him first, anyway.

Watching a World Series game with my dad was going to be fun.

I remember it drizzling on the ride from my parent's house to Philly. Weather reports were split on whether or not they'd get the game in.

One station on the radio kept mentioning the rules for it to be a regulation game, as if that was all they were aiming for.

Just get the game in.

The rain let up and we got to see the game. Nosebleed seats didn't dampen the game, either. The field looked waterlogged but they were going to play.

The Phillies had Tommy Greene starting against Todd Stottlemyre of the Blue Jays.

Toronto scored three runs in the top of the first. The Phillies came back with four in the bottom of the inning, all on four walks and a triple.

Philly scored two more runs in the bottom of the second with a Lenny Dykstra home run. 6-3 Phillies.

The Blue Jays got the lead back in the top of the third with four runs on four hits to make it 7-6. Tommy Greene was pulled after 2 ⅓ innings for Roger Mason.

In the bottom of the fourth the Phillies tied it off of Al Leiter. 7-7.

In the fifth the Phillies got to Leiter with homers from Darren Daulton and Dykstra again. Five runs scored before Leiter was pulled for Tony Castillo. Philly took a commanding 12-7 lead.

Top of the sixth the Blue Jays scored two runs against David West. 12-9 Phillies lead.

Philly scored a run in the bottom of the inning to make it 13-9 and another run in the seventh to widen the lead to 14-9.

Top of the eighth inning.

Larry Anderson gives up a run and is replaced by Wild Thing Mitch Williams, who Phillies fans loved that year. Up until this game.

He gave up five runs on three hits and the Blue Jays took the lead, 15-14.

That was it for the Phillies, who came up short in the eighth and ninth, with Duane Ward getting the save for the Blue Jays.

It was a monumental game even if I was rooting for the Phillies in this one.

There were some new World Series records set in this one, too: longest game at four hours and fourteen minutes; most runs scored by a losing team with fourteen; and most total runs scored in a single game with twenty-nine.

I remember Mitch Williams owned a bowling alley in New Jersey and it was on the news he'd been receiving death threats after the World Series. He became a goat for the Phillies after that game, which is a shame since he was a terrific player and a colorful pitcher who nearly fell off the mound after each pitch with his odd delivery.

I'm glad I got to share this with my dad and we still talk about it today.

Chapter 31: July 13 - 17. Away vs. Chattanooga Lookouts

July 13th

The Jumbo Shrimp lost, 5-4, to drop their record to 11-10 in the second half.

Reliever Daniel Schlereth blew a save in the bottom of the ninth and took the loss. He allowed two runs on two hits with two walks in ⅓ of an inning.

Starter Matt Tomshaw pitched a good game but came away empty-handed. He went seven innings and allowed only three runs on five hits. He had a walk and six strikeouts. After giving up the runs in the first inning he coasted the last six he pitched.

Instead of both hitting home runs in this game, John Norwood and Brian Anderson both got triples.

July 14th

Jacksonville lost, 9-3, and are now 11-11 in the second half. Overall they're 41-51, ten games under .500 on the season. I still have faith they can put together a few wins and make a nice run at the playoffs.

Starter Trevor Richards, just promoted back from Jupiter, had his first loss, going four innings while giving up five runs, four of them earned, on ten hits and two strikeouts. Joe Gunkel came on in relief but didn't fare much better in two innings, giving up three runs. He looked solid in his first inning of work, striking out all three batters he faced.

John Norwood continued his torrid hitting pace with his fifteenth home run of the season in the third.

Pitcher Daniel Schlereth was promoted to New Orleans.

July 15th

Another loss, this time 7-0. In all fairness, the Lookouts are on fire so far this year. They have an 18-5 record in the second half and are 60-33 overall.

Starter Mike Kickham worked four innings and allowed three runs on six hits. He struck out four and took the loss, his third in a row. He drops to 5-7.

The Jumbo Shrimp are still winless in road series this year in ten tries and it was the ninth time they were shutout.

Third baseman Brian Anderson was promoted to New Orleans, which we knew was going to happen. The bad part is we could really use his bat in the lineup right now. The team hasn't been hitting with any authority lately, relying on one or two players to have a good game instead of winning by team hitting effort.

First baseman Dustin Geiger was promoted from Jupiter to take the roster spot.

I talked to Dustin during the season.

How has being in the Marlins organization been different?

"It's good. I like it so far. I came over from the Cubs. It's a great mindset with both organizations. Both affiliates are here in Florida, which is nice. Being from Florida it is nice being able to have my parents drive up and down to see me. There's no big difference. Still a winning mentality. The goal is still the same. Get to the Big Leagues. Compete on that level and win a World Series. I watched the Cubs do it last year. I know the mentality that went into that and I tried to bring it with me."

How is it playing against guys you used to play with?

"That was a lot of fun. Mark Johnson is the manager for Tennessee this year, a team I played on in '14 and '15. He was my manager in extended spring training back when I was 19 years old in Arizona. It's nice seeing some of those guys. The players who were in Low-A when I was in Double-A. It was fun to reunite and play against them."

Is there motivation there?

"Every time somebody plays against their former team there's an extra effort, I think. I never had any negative being with the Cubs. I got released but I never held a grudge. That's just baseball. You have that little extra fire and you compete a little bit more."

Beginning of the season, where did you think you'd be?

"You try not to worry about it too much. You can't control it no matter what. The goal out of spring

training was to start in Double-A. They decided it was better for me to start in Jupiter and I was more than happy to go down there. I wanted to compete. Grateful for a jersey on my back. Just being back in an affiliate after being out of baseball for a couple of years was great. After the Cubs released me in '15 it was a long journey. Lots of different states. A lot of different teams in independent baseball. I was just grateful to break spring training with a job. Being able to compete in Jupiter was nice. Smoke Randel, our manager, was great. I fell into a leadership role as one of the older guys. It was a great experience. Our chaplain leader, George Buckland, is a wonderful person. I talked to him recently just to catch up. We talked about where I am right now and how grateful I am. We talked about God in our lives. The relationships I made in Jupiter are ones I'll have for the rest of my life."

Does seeing former MLB ballplayers in the independent leagues get you down?

"No, not at all. One of my teammates was Brent Clevlen, he played four years in the Majors with the Tigers and the Braves. He's one of those guys who's had life experiences I'm about to go through. Guys who are married and raising a family while playing baseball. The life aspect of this. It's not a negative in any way. We're all fighting to get back to an affiliate. There are some guys who go overseas to play. Japan. Taiwan. Korea. Mexico. Wherever. You go where you need to go to get back to the Majors. It was baseball. It was competitive. The different thing about independent ball is there are no levels to the organization. Your one goal on the field is to win the

championship in your league. As opposed to here, where you sometimes get caught up in yourself with the goal of getting to the Big Leagues. There's nothing wrong with it. Just a different mindset. The ultimate goal is to win at the Big League level. Indy ball is a win-now mentality."

How was it when you knew the Marlins were interested in you?

"I was ecstatic. Brett West, the assistant director in player development for the Marlins, called me back in December. I was about to go give lessons to some of my travel ball kids. We talked for about fifteen minutes. He told me what his idea for me in the organization was. He told me they weren't going to bring me in just to sit on the bench. That was huge to hear because there are so many guys that come out of independent ball who are fighting for jobs. Fighting for playing time. There are these other little things that get in the way of just playing the game. So me being able to come in here was amazing. When I went down to Jupiter I was the everyday guy. I had zero complaints. I was playing every day and that's the only way to get better. I'd rather be down there playing every day instead of sitting on the bench in Triple-A. If you're playing once every five days there's no development. You're not going to go anywhere. Coming to Double-A and splitting time with Taylor Ard at first base, luckily we'll have some series against American league teams so we'll have a DH. We can get more playing time. I'm just excited to help the team in any way."

What's the relationship with Taylor Ard?

"We're fine. We're great. We talk in the clubhouse and joke around just like anyone else. There's no hostility. Obviously our goal is the same. It pushes each of us a little bit more. He's a big corner guy. He has some power."

Goal for the season?

"To stay healthy. Compete every day and play through the end of the season. Make sure I'm on-time at the plate and putting in good swings. Good at-bats. Not giving anything away. Try to take advantage of every opportunity Randy Ready gives me."

I'm enjoying the addition of Dustin on the team already and I haven't seen him play a game yet. He's friendly, always smiling and upbeat. He has absolute faith he can accomplish his goals and it's infectious.

July 16th

Another loss, this time 5-2. Starter Chris Mazza is now 1-6 with the loss. He gave up three runs on seven hits. Walked two. Went five innings.

At least the bats seemed to come alive in the beginning of the game. John Norwood had an RBI single to break the Jumbo Shrimp out of their scoreless inning slump. Braxton Lee scored Austin Dean on a fielder's choice in the second.

Unfortunately the Lookout pitching then shut down the Jumbo Shrimp for the rest of the game. They left twelve men on base and hit a dismal 1-for-12 with runners in scoring position.

Lefty Dillon Peters was sent down to Jupiter but he should be back in Jacksonville in no time.

July 17th

Maybe this game will be the one they look back on as the one that swung the momentum for the second half. Fingers crossed.

The Jumbo Shrimp won, 9-6 after trailing 6-0 early in the game. They came back to score nine unanswered runs and take the win, their biggest comeback of the season.

Starter Omar Bencomo gave up the six runs in four innings on six hits, including a grand slam, and walked three with five strikeouts. It looked like this would be another Jumbo Shrimp loss. Joe Gunkel came in and promptly pitched two scoreless innings and eventually got the win. Tayron Guerrero went 1 ⅔ and struck out two for the hold. Clayton Mortensen finished it up for his fourth save of the season.

On the hitting side of things, the Jumbo Shrimp came alive. They scored one in the fourth, five runs in the fifth and three in the sixth.

Braxton Lee, Austin Dean and Rodrigo Vigil collected three hits apiece. Dustin Geiger and David Vidal had two each. Dustin also had four RBI's as the designated hitter. I knew I liked this guy.

The team is on its way back to Jacksonville and will get an off day tomorrow. Hopefully it will allow them to regroup.

Chapter 32: July 19 - 23. Home vs. Tennessee Smokies

July 19th

This was a big home win to start the series, 10-6. Starter Matt Tomshaw got an easy win, going six innings and only giving up two runs in the fourth inning. By this point the Jumbo Shrimp offense had scored eight runs.

Catcher Cam Maron had five RBI's with a homerun, his fourth, and a single. First baseman Dustin Geiger went 3-for-3 and hit his first homer of the season.

David Vidal and John Norwood both had two hits as well.

3,384 fans and a lot of dogs saw a great game as it was Canines and Crustaceans on a Wednesday night. One thing I will say about this team's staff is they know how to throw a party. The contests and in-between inning fun is always getting the crowd going and you can see the smiles on their faces as they walk through the crowds and interact with the fans.

Lefty Mike Kickham was promoted to New Orleans and swapped places with lefty Victor Payano.

July 20th

Tonight, every time a Jumbo Shrimp pitcher got a strikeout it would raise $5,300 thanks to Fifth Third Bank for Stand Up To Cancer.

They fanned thirteen.

Add 5,898 fans in the ballpark for an added $5,898 and they raised $74,798.

The Smokies won, 9-3, but it was almost an afterthought for the fans with all the good vibes tonight.

Starter Trevor Richards struck out nine Smokies, including seven in a row. Tyler Higgins struck out one and Victor Payano had three. The thirteen total strikeouts was two shy of the season high. They picked a great night to do get close, too.

Highlights for the offense included first baseman Dustin Geiger, going 1-for-3 with an RBI. He's hitting .474 since his promotion from Jupiter.

July 21st

Another win in dramatic fashion, and it wasn't even because of John Norwood this time. Shortstop Chris Diaz hit an infield single that scored third baseman David Vidal in the bottom of the ninth for the 3-2 win. 8,454 fans were still cheering when the Friday night fireworks began.

Starter Joe Gunkel looked impressive to start the game, retiring the first nine he faced in six shutout innings. Clayton Mortensen, newcomer Joe Quijada just promoted from Jupiter, Andy Beltre and Jeff Kinley kept them in the game until two outs in the top of the ninth when Severino Gonzalez came in and gave up a game-tying sacrifice fly for a blown save. When the team won dramatically the bottom of the inning he picked up the win.

Besides lefty Jose Quijada's promotion, righty Tyler Kinley was also called up from Jupiter. Righty Tayron Guerrero was shipped up to New Orleans.

July 22nd

Rain. Lots of rain. We'll play two tomorrow if the weather holds.

I had a chance to talk to Braxton Lee during the season and he's another humble player with a smile etched on his face.

Is there a big adjustment from switching teams mid-year?

"Not much of an adjustment switching teams because it's in the same league. After last year, when it wasn't so hot for me, I had to learn from my mistakes and cope with them better this year. I hit .209 in 2016, which is not impressive. I had to grow up a little bit and find out what I needed to do to succeed. It's still hard but being able to come from last year and what I did then has really helped me throughout this year. If I get into any struggles this year I can look back and make quick adjustments that have really helped me. I just think last year, having such an off year for me, has helped me to adjust this year."

What's your off season like after a bad year?

"I went in with a positive mindset because after last year it was the worst feeling in the world. I told myself no excuses this year. This is all on you. I went into it mindful of the decisions I was making on the field. Every day play hard and leave no regrets on the field. Having an uplifting attitude towards everything. After last year I just tried to relax. Not dwell on it. I did some hunting and fishing. Just get my mind off of all that for awhile. Coming into spring training with the Rays and doing my best every day was the goal. I came in prepared to do positive things this year."

Where were you when you heard about the trade?

"I didn't hear anything until it actually happened. The day I got traded I ended up getting tossed from the game in the fourth inning. I came in and deleted all my social media but I had a friend tell me to check something out so I re-downloaded Twitter. I was scrolling through to see what I got ejected for, honestly, and then I see my name. I'm like... what? I tell my clubhouse manager I think I'm about to get traded. Thirty minutes later I was traded. My manager calls me in and he's like, 'hey, good luck, blah blah blah.' That was it. I had no clue. I didn't think the day before it would happen. That day it happened."

How is it to come to a new organization after being in the Rays system your entire career?

"The good part being traded from Montgomery to Jacksonville is we only had to play them one more time. I got to go see them and that was good. Baseball is just a big family. I played against a bunch of the guys on Jacksonville before. Guys who were in

Jupiter when I was in Charlotte. So I knew them already. Now being on a team with them is easy. I thought coming over it would be a bigger deal than it was. But coming over and playing with these guys and seeing who they actually were was great. They've accepted me with open arms. I can't thank them enough. They've made it easier on me."

Who were your baseball idols growing up?

"Growing up I remember Ichiro. As a kid I was amazed how he could get a hit at will. I was that lefty kid who hit all the time, eight years old into high school. It's mostly been outfielders like Jim Edmonds. I mean, I love watching Mike Trout. Guys who are an inspiration. If they're doing it I want to do it. I never had favorite teams growing up. I like the players who go out and play hard every day."

Braxton Lee is a guy who plays hard every day and his breakout year so far is turning heads. This is one of those special players who breaks out after some adjustments and will be heading to Miami sooner than later.

In transaction news, pitcher Clayton Mortensen was put on the 7-Day DL with a triceps strain.

July 23rd

A split of a doubleheader put the Jumbo Shrimp into a tie for first place in the South Division.

Game one starter Chris Mazza pitched seven innings, striking out eight while giving up four hits and four walks. He left in a scoreless game. Tyler

Kinley pitched the last two innings in relief but took the loss, giving up both runs in the 2-0 loss.

Lone highlight for me was John Norwood going 2-for-4 with his 10th double of the season.

In game two the Jumbo Shrimp fared better, winning 3-1. Starter Omar Bencomo (now 5-4) got the win with five scoreless innings. He allowed two hits and struck out three.

Severino Gonzalez pitched the seventh inning for his third save of the season.

Second baseman KC Serna was sent down from New Orleans and center fielder Yefri Perez was put on the 7-Day DL with a heel contusion.

Chapter 33: Baseball trip with dad

My dad and I were hanging out watching a baseball game on TV. It must've been in late summer 2015 and we started talking about some of the games we'd gone to, some of which I talk about in this very book.

We'd hit most of the stadiums up and down the East Coast. We'd been to all of the stadiums between Boston and Tampa, but a few stadiums I'd never been to. Like Wrigley Field.

That was it. We both got excited. We were going to take a baseball trip and see the stadiums we either hadn't been to or they'd been updated since our last visit.

When my wife, mom and daughter came home from shopping we told them about the trip and how much fun we'd all have on it. A week or two traveling in my dad's van seeing the sights.

It was quickly decided (by my wife, mom and daughter) that this would be a perfect father-son bonding trip.

And so we planned. For months. Looking at the upcoming schedule and mapping a route that made sense to hit everything we wanted to.

The initial idea was to hit ten games in ten days but that fell apart when certain teams weren't at home during our trip. Because of my book signing schedule and convention dates we only had a brief window for next June to travel.

Games in Pittsburgh and Minnesota were ruled out. They'd be too far away from the other games to make sense driving. We cancelled Atlanta since we could go there anytime we wanted.

Since my dad's birthday was June 21st I made sure we had a Tigers game that day. We'd base all the other games around it, and add in a few other stops along the way, too.

As a gift to my dad I paid for the trip. Tickets, hotels and gas. All he'd need to do was bring some money for eating at the different ballparks.

By the time the trip was upon us we'd talked it to death. My wife goofed on me because for months, nearly every day my dad would call me with another idea for the trip.

Sunday June 19th 2016

These games weren't about who the home team was playing. It wasn't about who won or anything other than seeing the game with my dad and eating ballpark food and enjoying the atmosphere.

We drove from Florida to Cleveland to begin our trip and took in an afternoon Indians game versus the White Sox. Progressive Field (I still called it Jacobs Field or The Jake) was great to see a game in. Another thing we didn't worry about on this trip was expensive seats. We just wanted to sit in the bleachers or upper deck and enjoy the game.

For this first game we got great seats down the left field line. We wandered the stadium and ate. A lot. I got to see Terry Francona before the game doing interviews between the baseball stadium and the Quicken Loans Arena next door, which was set up with booths and a sound system because the Cleveland Cavaliers were playing that night in San Francisco against the Golden State Warriors for the NBA Title.

My dad enjoys gambling so we'd spent a few hours before the baseball game in the casino a couple of blocks away. I do not gamble so I caught up on work emails and people-watched.

After the Indians game we went back to the casino. Our goal was to stay in town since tomorrow we had no game and see the Rock And Roll Hall of Fame down the street.

Those plans were crushed when the Cavs won the title and suddenly thousands of ecstatic fans filled the streets. And the casino.

We decided to get out of Cleveland and head to Canton, where we hoped it was a bit quieter.

Monday June 20th 2016

We visited the Football Hall of Fame. I'd never been and it was amazing. We spent a large part of the day wandering the rooms. I grew up an Oakland Raiders fan. My brother is a New York Jets fan. My mom loves the New England Patriots and my dad is a Green Bay Packers fan.

Maybe someday I'll write a book about the football fights we all had growing up.

I got to hear stories from my dad about growing up a Packers fan in New Jersey. I could relate as a Red Sox fan doing the same thing.

My dad spent a lot of time at the various Packers sections.

We left late in the afternoon to get some food and head towards Detroit.

Tuesday June 21st 2016

It was dad's birthday. Sixty-six years old and he can still walk faster than I can, especially when we are in a casino.

We arrived in Detroit several hours before game time. I bought two tickets for the Comerica Park tour, which was fantastic. We were with a small group and I could see how happy my dad was when we got to walk onto the field and sit in the dugout.

The history of the place is great, even if it opened in 2000 and obviously isn't the original Tigers Stadium we'd seen Mark Fidrych pitch in forty years ago.

After the tour we walked a few blocks to a casino. I worked on my phone and dad gambled for awhile. Then it was back to the stadium to see the game.

Since it was his birthday I made sure we got better seats, a few rows up near the first base line. He got to see Verlander pitch and win the game, too.

Then it was off to Chicago after the game.

Wednesday June 22nd 2016

It was raining. Heavily at times. We pulled into Chicago and it was absolute chaos around Wrigley Field. I imagine it usually is on game day, even when it looks like the game will be canceled.

We had no contingency plan for a rained out game. Tomorrow was a free day, the last of the trip, so we started thinking about the logistics of needing to stay instead of heading to our next destination after the game.

Luckily the rain slowed enough and they opened the gates. Our seats were all the way upstairs down the first base line. After a delay while they got the field back in shape and my dad went to get food and drink for us since I am afraid of heights (and a wimp) and felt like I was going to fall forward and hit the field, even though we were several rows back.

The St. Louis Cardinal defeated the Cubs with Jake Arrieta getting the loss.

I was just happy to finally see a game at Wrigley Field.

Despite the rain it was a great day.

We left the Taco Bell parking lot (which had become a game parking lot) and headed towards Wisconsin.

Thursday June 23rd

We checked into an actual motel. Quaint and clean, they still used actual keys for the doors. While my dad walked over to the motel restaurant I did some work. Later, after we'd returned to the room, I walked across the street to an actual diner and ate like I hadn't eaten in weeks.

Hey, I'm from New Jersey. We like our diners.

We drove over to Lambeau Field. Home of the Green Bay Packers.

Another exciting stop on our trip and my dad was grinning as we took the tour of the stadium, hanging out in a skybox and walking on the sidelines on the field.

What an awesome day.

Friday June 24th 2016

We got to Milwaukee and checked into our hotel. It used a swipe card. After settling in and taking naps we jumped back in the van and headed to Miller Park.

The parking lot was huge and we parked about halfway down and took the long walk to the stadium. The Washington Nationals were in town.

Our seats were all the way upstairs, eye level with Bernie Brewer. If there was a home run from the Brewers we'd have a great view to see him sliding down to the lower level of his dugout.

We could see the Bob Uecker statue behind section 422, only a few sections away from us. The stadium, built in 2001, was modern and had great views of the field no matter where you sat.

They also sold their beer in plastic Brewers mugs. I didn't drink any but during this trip I'd promised my wife a couple of things from each stadium: a magnet for our fridge and at least one souvenir cup. As if we didn't have enough Jumbo Shrimp ones already.

Suffice it to say I came home with magnets from every stadium and several dozen plastic cups from every game.

After the game we drove back towards Chicago.

Saturday June 25th 2016

It was a day game in Chi-town to see the White Sox at Guaranteed Rate Field. We sat directly in the sun in right field. It got so hot my dad took a walk and waved at me from a section a few over and under the overhang and in the shade so I joined him.

Much better.

The Blue Jays were in town.

I ate way too much food and drank several sodas in souvenir cups.

This was a modern stadium even though it was built in 1991. I wondered what seeing a game at the old Comiskey Park would've been like.

We were nearing the end of our trip but having a great time.

After the game we were off to Cincinnati.

Sunday June 26th 2016

We arrived in Cincinnati very early in the morning and so my dad found the nearest casino. We hung around there in the air conditioning and he had the bright idea to walk the dozen blocks to the day game and leave the van in the casino parking garage.

City blocks. In the heat. Did I mention I'm on the bigger side? As in fat.

I think I shed a few pounds trying to keep pace with my dad, who nearly runs when he goes anywhere.

We got to the game, which happened to be Pete Rose Day where they retired his number 14 with a ceremony before the game.

Our seats were in the left field upper deck with the sun a few feet from my bald head. Did I mention the heat already? I drank quite a few sodas during the actual game, which was against the Padres.

The stadium had a great design and the view was spectacular, even if it was a bit too hot for me. And I live in Florida.

Afterwards we headed back to the casino, which I'm positive had been moved an additional ten city blocks while we were in Great American Ball Park.

Feeling like we had a great week of games and fun, we got into the van, cranked the air conditioning and headed back to Florida and home.

This will always be a trip I will remember sharing with my dad.

Especially when I'm drinking out of a White Sox or Indians plastic cup.

Chapter 34: July 25 - 29. Away vs. Mississippi Braves

July 24th

During the travel day to Pearl, Mississippi lefty Dillon Peters was promoted from Jupiter and lefty Victor Payano was promoted to New Orleans.

July 25th

The Jumbo Shrimp lost 3-2, on the wrong end of a walk-off home run by M-Braves center fielder Connor Lien. Reliever Severino Gonzalez gave it up and took the loss.

Starter Matt Tomshaw went seven innings, allowing only two runs on six hits. He struck out seven in the no-decision.

Starter Mike Soroka of the M-Braves also went seven innings, giving up one run on six hits. He struck out six. He's one of the players high on the Atlanta Braves prospect list and a player who should keep moving up in their system.

I listened to the game while in Atlanta with my wife, who was doing actual work while I listened to baseball games on my laptop. This is the life.

I was getting excited because in three days we'd be in Pearl Mississippi for two games cheering the Jumbo Shrimp on. It would be our second trip of the season to see them on the road and we'd follow it up with going to Biloxi to see them take on the Shuckers the two days after.

July 26th

Starter Trevor Richards pitched seven scoreless innings with only five hits, a walk and six strikeouts to get the 3-0 victory. Tyler Kinley picked up his third save.

Third baseman David Vidal hit his fifth home run of the season in the second inning to take the 2-0 lead. In the eighth catcher Rodrigo Vigil had an RBI single for the only other run in this game.

Nothing against the M-Braves, but they are a struggling team this year. This is the team the Jumbo Shrimp need to beat every series. Winning this second game is great but now they need to keep it going if they want to stay in the hunt for the playoffs. Just my own two cents.

July 27th

The Jumbo Shrimp got the win, 2-1, in another low-scoring game. At least when the team isn't hitting like crazy the pitching is keeping them in the games. It's been the difference between the first half and second half so far for the team.

Starter Dillon Peters went five innings, only yielding a run on six hits. It's good to see this Marlins prospect back on the mound after being out since mid-April. Tyler Higgins pitched two scoreless innings and picked up the win, his third of the year. Andy Beltre pitched a scoreless inning and then so did Tyler Kinley, who picked up his fourth save.

KC Serna, playing second base, went 2-for-3.

It hit 91 degrees and it looks like when we go to the game tomorrow it will be around the same.

July 28th

It was, indeed, 91 degrees at game time. 3,532 (including me, my wife and daughter) took in a night game. Yes, it was still hot. We sat right behind the visitor dugout and there weren't too many other people in our section. I'm sure we looked completely out of place in our Jumbo Shrimp gear.

There is netting on top of the dugout so we wouldn't get hit with a foul ball. First baseman Dustin Geiger would throw the ball at the net as he came off the field and at first my wife thought he was throwing the ball at her.

When I told him this later in the season he laughed. He liked to bounce the ball off the net and catch it as he ran into the dugout.

It was during these two games in Mississippi I did about half of the player interviews. A huge thanks to Roger Hoover for setting them up and making me feel at home. He really went out of his way to make sure whatever player I wanted to chat with was available, if possible.

One of the players I talked to was tonight's starter, Joe Gunkel.

Does the Mississippi heat affect your game?

"There's a point and time in the game when you're really hot. Really tired. Once you get over that hump it is cruise control from there. You get really exhausted and your body takes over. By the third or fourth inning the heat starts to get to me but once I get past that I'm good to go. It wasn't even hot. The humidity was brutal," Joe said.

He's right. It's not the heat. It's the humidity.

My daughter decides her new favorite player is second baseman Alex Yarbrough. Not for his hitting or fielding but because he's cute. Her previous favorite was third baseman Brian Anderson, who moved up to New Orleans and was enjoying a nice run so far. She says he was cute, too. I don't bother talking to her about his major league potential or his great glove-work on the hot corner or his fourteen homers before he was promoted.

We meet usher Teddie, a man in his late sixties, who's eyeing my Jumbo Shrimp hat. When we tell him we made the trip from Jacksonville to see the team his eyes light up. He's a longtime baseball fan and enjoys working and watching the game.

When I mention the stadiums we've visited and some plans for next season involving seeing a few of the other stadiums in the league, he nods appreciatively.

"When I was fifty years old I planned the dream baseball trip of a lifetime. It would be for the entire month of July. I took the month off of work. Planned out every day, making sure I could see as many ballgames as possible. I came home to tell my wife, who told me she was pregnant," Teddie said with a grin. *"Sixteen years of marriage with no kids. She was told she couldn't have children. Can you believe it? Our son was born the July we were supposed to take the trip so I never went."*

Teddie smiles when he tells the story. I can see he wouldn't trade the way it happened for anything in the world, even a dream baseball trip. I wonder how many other fans seated in his section he's told over the years.

The stadium is a throwback to what I used to think a minor league stadium was: simple design but still impressive. It has that feel of old school baseball. I was surprised to find out the stadium was built in 2005, although I guess in terms of sports complexes that is pretty old nowadays with so many new stadiums being built. All in all a great place to see a game.

And what a game we saw, as David Vidal hit a solo homer in the ninth inning and the Jumbo Shrimp took it, 4-3. He'd also hit one back in the third inning. He has seven on the year.

As mentioned, Joe Gunkel got the start. He went seven innings, giving up two runs on two hits with four strikeouts. Severino Gonzalez came into the game in relief and blew a save opportunity with one run on two hits. He's done this before.

When Vidal hit the go-ahead homer in the ninth Gonzalez picked up the win, his fifth of the season. Jeff Kinley pitched a scoreless ninth for his first save.

Can't wait to come back tomorrow and hope to see another win. Now we're off to find somewhere local to eat.

Righty Omar Bencomo was promoted to New Orleans and the Miami Marlins made a trade coming up to the deadline, trading closer AJ Ramos to the New York Mets for minor leaguers Merandy Gonzalez, a right-handed pitcher, and Ricardo Cespedes, an outfielder.

With only a few days left until the trade deadline, I'm keeping one eye on my phone to see if any other trades materialize.

July 29th

Day starts with rain. Lots of kids in the hotel and we can't figure out why this is a vacation destination. The mall? The movies? The baseball stadium? I need to ask someone who works at the hotel because I'm curious. Also nosy.

But since I'm lazier than anything I don't ask.

I spend the next few hours looking at the weather and trade rumor sites back and forth between playing Facebook sports games and talking with my wife and daughter, who seem reluctant to get out of their beds on such a gloomy day. They spend their time on their phones. Most likely also playing Facebook games.

Too nervous as I head over to Trustmark Park with my wife (my daughter opted to stay in bed and play Facebook games) to interview a few of the Jumbo Shrimp players for this book. Will they look at me as an outsider or a pitifully fat old man whose best days are long behind?

Okay, I don't really get that dramatic. I am nervous to chat with them, though. Not sure why. I've done hundreds of interviews in the last few years, but mostly with fellow authors or podcasters. Filmmakers. Actors. Actresses. Pro wrestlers. Musicians. Never anyone in sports.

I worried for nothing. Like I said yesterday, Roger Hoover is friendly and easygoing. He sets me up in a quiet area for the interviews and my wife hangs in the background to hear what the players have to say.

Then it's off to lunch and back to the hotel until game time.

Trade rumors: the Cubs are interested in Marlins catcher A.J. Ellis, which immediately makes me think of the subsequent catcher moves if this one is done in the next couple of days. Austin Nola, who we'd followed as a Jumbo Shrimp, was currently up in Triple-A. Cam Maron and Rodrigo Vigil were the backstops in Jacksonville. My wife was a big fan of Cam Maron, especially for his name. Chris Hoo, who'd spent time with the Jumbo Shrimp after coming off the DL for awhile, had been sent down to the Jupiter Hammerheads.

Also rumored to be traded but less likely given his contract is second baseman Dee Gordon, son of former Red Sox closer Tom Gordon.

I love this time of year.

By game time the weather is playing nice. It's in the mid-80's and there is actually a breeze. It feels so much nicer than last night. We're still sitting right behind the visitor's dugout.

Usher Teddie, still smiling from last night, makes me an offer I can't refuse: he wants to trade a Mississippi Braves hat for my black Jumbo Shrimp cap. He says he collects them from opposing team fans whenever possible but he's never run into a Jumbo Shrimp fan this far west of Jacksonville.

I agree, knowing I'll need to buy a new one as soon as we return home. It's also the only one I brought with me on the trip.

I have this weird rule (maybe it's not too weird but my wife thinks so) where I won't wear a jersey or team shirt paired with a team hat. If I wear a Red Sox shirt I'll put on a Shrimp hat or vice versa. Never both of the same team. I might wear a Project Entertainment Network shirt (my podcast network I own) or a non-sports cap. To me it's what the players are allowed to do on the field. They earned it. I'm just a fan.

And I'm weird, according to my wife.

During the game I actually get out of my seat and wander to check out the stadium. This might be my last visit so I want to make sure I don't miss anything.

I'm particularly enamored by their Hall of Fame wall. Maybe they call it a Wall of Fame. Who knows? Of course I pointed out the players who played for the M-Braves but had played with the Red Sox at some point in their career, like Craig Kimbrel and Jarrod Saltalamacchia.

My wife bid on and won a signed bat, too.

And we watched a baseball game.

Unfortunately the Jumbo Shrimp were shutout, 4-0. Starter Chris Mazza is now 1-7 with the loss. He's been pitching better than his record reflects, but it's been an up and down struggle. When you give up four runs in five innings you can only hope your offense will pick you up, which didn't happen tonight.

Third baseman David Vidal hit a double and brought his average up to .299.

Hopefully a change of scenery will do the team good, as they begin a series in Biloxi tomorrow night.

We'd be leaving to make the drive to Biloxi ourselves.

Chapter 35: July 30 - August 3. Away vs. Biloxi Shuckers

July 30th

I wake up in Pearl and frantically search for trades being made by the Red Sox or Marlins. Nothing. Not even new rumors this morning. This is unacceptable. I live for this stuff.

We meet my dad at the casino. He's in town and got us a beautiful comp'd room to stay in while in Biloxi. Since he still doesn't have a cell phone or would know what to do with it, I fill him in on all the baseball trade rumors.

He is not happy about the Tigers, rumored to be trading left-hander Justin Wilson and catcher Mike Avila to the Cubs for prospects.

We check into our room, which is amazing, and I continue to monitor trade rumors until game time.

The stadium isn't far at all and we find parking in a lot between two buildings, where the guy running it welcomes us back even though we've never been there before. Not a friendly welcome back in general, but because he actually thinks we're there all the time and starts chatting with us as we walk away.

I guess I have that face or we have that look? No idea. He's nice but I want to get inside and watch a game.

A woman on the concourse at MGM Park is wearing the same Jumbo Shrimp shirt my wife is wearing. She's walking around with a huge smile on her face.

When she sees us in our gear she gives me a high-five.

"Are you from Jacksonville?" I ask.

She shakes her head. "My son is playing on the Jacksonville team. Braxton Lee."

I'd had the pleasure of interviewing Braxton the previous day in Pearl. I tell her she raised a great kid and she thanks me.

"This is like a home game for him. So many of his friends and family are here to cheer Braxton on." He's from nearby Picayune.

She's right. Anytime he gets up to bat or makes a play in the outfield it sounds like the population of Picayune is in the stands cheering for him.

The stadium is nice. One of the newer ones from what they tell me. We're sitting a little higher than usual but still near the visitor's dugout. Maybe Randy Ready will catch a glimpse of us and shake his head again.

As to the actual game… the Jumbo Shrimp lost, this time 4-3.

Starter Matt Tomshaw was the losing pitcher, giving up four runs on ten hits.

Braxton Lee must've loved having so many fans cheering him on because he went 3-for-5 with two RBI's.

July 31st

Trade deadline is today. I look at the app on my phone then back to the laptop, as if the information will be different or one device will scoop it before the other. My bet is on the phone if it goes down.

Mets righty Addison Reed is going to the Red Sox for three prospects. Maybe. Still a rumor at this point. The Bosox would give up Gerson Bautista, Jamie Callahan and Stephen Nogosek, all relievers. Reed would be an expensive setup man for Kimbrel.

I'm not seeing much about the Marlins other than the typical guesses on who might be traded and to what team.

Pitcher Tyler Higgins and I talked about the trade deadline and also Braxton Lee.

We're right before the trading deadline. Marlins are a seller at this point. AJ Ramos was traded yesterday. Do you follow it and wonder if a spot is going to open up for you above?

"I guess you can. There are some guys who do worry about it. I just need to keep playing. Thinking about it isn't going to do anything for me. I don't think it benefits anybody. If it happens it happens and if it doesn't it doesn't. Nothing in my daily routine will affect it. No sense in worrying yourself about it. You can control what you do on the field and try to do the best you can and make the right plays to get moved up and up. All you can do," Tyler said.

A guy like Braxton Lee is traded over midseason. How does that affect you as a pitcher?

"He's good. He's one of the better defensive outfielders I've played with. But just for the sake of noting it: he's actually 0 for 4 against me. He doesn't hit me. I made sure he knew that when he came over. I wrote it on a ball and put it in his locker." Tyler can't stop grinning as he tells me this, looking around and hoping Braxton is within earshot. *"But seriously, it's really nice to have him on our team. He's leading the league in average. Defensively he's unbelievable. If it gets by him it was a hit anyway. It's really good to have that guy switch fences."*

I can't wait for the game tonight but I also need to see the big trades that will reshape the Red Sox and Marlins…

...and the MLB Trading Deadline is over and done with and it's a bust as far as I'm concerned but a relief to many players who aren't going anywhere. Players in the Red Sox minor league system aren't in danger of being an extra piece in a potential trade and the Marlins minor leaguers aren't worried about losing their roster spot to a hotshot player received when one of their Major Leaguers was dealt. Now everyone can focus on the next month or two of baseball, right?

It's another good night for baseball regardless of who wins or loses. I just love being at the game. My wife and I spend a lot of time between innings people-watching. Since I'm a writer I make up elaborate stories about people and sometimes they make it into a future story.

Two older gentlemen in front of us talk baseball. Arthur is full of stories. He tells us about the Washington Senators being in Biloxi in the early

1930's for spring training. They practiced at the old Biloxi Stadium, which is now part of Keesler Air Force Base. He tells a story about Franklin Delano Roosevelt telling a woman he was a Senator and she was disappointed to find out he meant a New York Senator in government and not a Washington Senator playing baseball.

Arthur's buddy is a Red Sox fan and he talks about being stationed in Baltimore and not wanting to leave the military until he saw as many Red Sox games as possible while he was there.

The people at the game are friendly. It seems like quite a few in our section are from out of town, taking a break from the casinos to see a ballgame.

We get to see a Jumbo Shrimp loss. 3-2. It feels like they either win or lose every game with this exact score.

Starter Trevor Richards is now 3-3. He went six innings and gave up three runs (two earned) on five hits. He set down the final fourteen Shuckers he faced in order.

Braxton Lee went 1-for-4 with a double and scored a run. The team scattered eight hits but hit into three double plays, killing any rally.

Righty Clayton Mortensen was activated from the disabled list.

August 1st

Another low-scoring loss, 2-1. Starter Dillon Peters went six innings, giving up both runs on three hits and two walks while striking out seven.

It looked like the offense was going to set the tone for this game early for the Jumbo Shrimp. John Norwood knocked in Austin Dean with an RBI single to take the early lead.

The Shuckers answered right back in the bottom of the second with a two-run homer.

That was the end of the power surge… in the game.

Downtown Biloxi itself had a power surge and it took nearly half an hour for the lights to come back on and the game commencing.

In the last five innings of the game the Jumbo Shrimp were sent down in order each time.

August 2nd

A massively lopsided loss, 13-0. Starter Joe Gunkel went four innings, giving up five runs (four earned) on nine hits including two home runs. Esmerling De La Rosa pitched two scoreless innings but then Clayton Mortensen, recently off the disabled list, gave up four runs on two hits and two walks and only recorded one out. Jose Quijada didn't do much better, recording two outs while giving up four runs on seven hits and a walk. KC Serna was pulled off the bench in relief. The infielder was their best pitcher of the night with a perfect inning.

On the other hand, the Jumbo Shrimp managed four scattered hits on the night. Maybe the Shuckers tired themselves out running the bases and will be lethargic tomorrow night?

August 3rd

Another low-scoring shutout game, 3-0. At least in this one the Jumbo Shrimp got the win. Starter Chris Mazza (now 2-7) went 8 ⅓ innings for the win. He gave up only two hits and walked three, striking out two. It was his first win since mid-May. Tyler Kinley came on for the last two outs of the ninth and his fifth save.

The Jumbo Shrimp didn't score until the sixth inning with two sacrifice flies. Dustin Geiger hit a solo homer in the ninth.

The win snapped a five-game losing streak for the Jumbo Shrimp.

Chapter 36: Jumbo Shrimp Staff Interviews II

A few more interviews with Jumbo Shrimp office staff and their stories.

David Ratz, Promotions & Special Events Manager

What is your job on a day to day basis?

"I'm in charge of the fun. Whether it's a theme night or promotional giveaway, I'm in charge of writing a script for everything that happens inside the stadium. Pretty much everything but the actual baseball game being played is in my hands. The fan experience. What jerseys the team is wearing to auction them off. If we're giving out bobbleheads. Plus, events in the stadium all year that don't involve baseball as well."

How far in advance are you planning these events?

"I'm already working on things for next season. It's constantly working ahead."

How long have you been in this job?

"This is my first year working with the Jumbo Shrimp. My wife and I were season ticket holders for

four seasons. I came over from Cox Media Group. I worked there for fourteen years. I did promotions for them. The work is similar but different."

Is it a group effort for new ideas?

"It's 100% a team effort. We have promo meetings and we bounce ideas off the wall. We see what we like and what we could make work. Just toss it out there and figure out how it can or can't work. One nice thing here is everyone contributes. I take all the input with help from other people and we decide what to do and how to execute it."

Are there certain promotions that have to be done between innings?

"Yeah, definitely. We look at it a bit differently. It is a minor league baseball game but we approach it like the actual baseball is secondary. You come for an evening out and you want to be entertained. If you happen to be a baseball fan that's awesome. We need to entertain between innings. During rain delays. A lot of those between-innings events are tied to sponsors, too. When you know what sponsors are coming in you can brainstorm ideas for events. Base a contest around their product."

So someone like Metro Diner comes in. How does that contest get put together?

"Metro Diner comes in and says they want to be a between-innings sponsor. So we came up with some ideas and went back and presented them. They said that was awesome. Now someone like The Law Offices of John M. Phillips came to us and said they wanted in with the weird laws on the screen and the four shoes promotion. He came to us. We build and

execute his idea. A lot depends on the sponsor and what they want to see."

Is there a rhyme or reason to when the promotions go off?

"There is no rhyme or reason for when we do certain events between innings. You try to mix it up. You have to remember, for about forty percent of the people through the gates that night, it's their first game. You also have the season ticket holders and weekend packages as well as returning fans, so you don't just want the same show every night. Sometimes it falls into that trap where you have to do it at a certain time because everything else that night is set. We do make an effort to move them around. If you have a promotion like Sweet Pete's, where you're giving away the best seats in the house, obviously you want to do that one early so the winners can enjoy those seats for the rest of the game. Giving that away in the eighth inning wouldn't be ideal. Setting the schedule for each game is a nice challenge. When you have seventy performances a year and someone like yourself sees sixty five or more games, you want to keep it fresh."

How many promotions are you spinning in and out?

"The between inning breaks are sold to sponsors on a yearly basis. We try to have three or four different ones for that sponsor so on a five-game homestand you see one or two twice but not the same one five nights in a row. An Applebee's trivia question will be a trivia question every night. A t-shirt toss will be a t-shirt toss every night. The ones

interactive with games we try to have a couple of alternatives."

What are some of them you've come up with yourself?

"The chicken and waffle one is my favorite one. I was home and thinking about it. I thought it would be fun. How can I create big waffle hands and throw chickens in the air? It's a signature dish Metro Diner is known for. That was the one I had the most fun with."

Ernest Hopkins, Director of Food & Beverage

What's your day to day like?

"On game day all the hard work and preparation is done. On game day I'm walking around, making sure everything is going as planned. Recheck the schedule. Recheck your orders. I look at attendance to see if there's an increase in numbers as far as expected attendance. I'm making sure everyone's in place."

What's the normal staffing?

"On an average game it's about twenty. On a bigger night, like Friday night with fireworks, the staff is over fifty to seventy-five people."

You have a rotating team coming in and out?

"Exactly. A bunch of part-time seasonal workers. We have over two hundred fifty employees. A lot have other jobs or other needs. We rotate different people in most days. There's no set crew every day."

How long have you been with the Jumbo Shrimp?

"This is my second year. Before this I was food & beverage manager at Jacksonville Veterans Memorial Arena."

What pulled you across the street?

"The new ownership. I applied over here because I saw a great opportunity to further my career. I feel like I made a great decision."

Is it a homestand to homestand basis you look at the numbers and orders?

"Every game is different. Every homestand is different. Every day there's someone new coming into the ballpark. It's not like a restaurant where you can know on Thursday we feed this many people, on Friday this many. Every week, every homestand is different. Weather also plays a very important part of this, too, being an outdoor facility."

Does a rain delay mean anything for bigger numbers?

"Not really. It depends on what inning it is. If it's the third or fourth inning people have probably eaten already. Past this inning you might see a bump in desserts. People don't usually storm the concession stands during a rain delay. With baseball, people coming in before the start of the game usually find their seats right before or right after they buy their food. A rain delay past the fourth inning you're pretty safe."

You're a baseball fan?

"Atlanta Braves. I grew up in Macon Georgia."

Ken Sparks, Usher on the third base side in sections 101 to 103

How long have you been here?

"This is my second year. I retired in 2014. In 2015 I spent my time going between Daytona (to see the Cubs and then Tortugas) and Jacksonville Suns games to see minor league baseball. I love to watch the game. When I saw the job fair in Jacksonville I thought it would be great to get a job here and they can pay me to watch baseball."

Growing up, what teams did you root for?

"I grew up in western Pennsylvania. Everyone's a Pittsburgh Pirates fan. I root for them but I'm actually an L.A. Dodgers fan. They had cool uniforms when I was a kid. When I was nine or ten Sandy Koufax was pitching. Great pitching teams in the 60's. I also root for anyone who plays the Yankees."

They put you in this section for a reason according to Clayton, because of the way the kids (and adults) bother the players in the dugout during the game.

"The owner of the Jumbo Shrimp wants this to be fun for everyone. As a kid I didn't get to go to many baseball games. When I did go I was in awe. Going to a game was the neatest thing to do. These kids are interested in baseball. They want to get a baseball from the players. They're excited about it. When I talk to the kids I realize this might be something they were truly looking forward to. I don't want to ruin that experience. My chief concern is safety. Keep them out of the aisles and blocking the view of others trying to watch the game. In between innings, as long as

they're behaving, I'm not going to say too much. When the inning starts I'm going to sit them down. I do it so they're not scared. They enjoy coming to the ballpark. It's a great experience for them."

How many games a year are you working?

"Last year I did sixty-four games. I won't do quite as many this year. They scheduled me fifty-five to sixty."

When you have the day off are you still checking to see how the Jumbo Shrimp are doing?

"I always check online to see how the team does. What the attendance is. Who had the big hits? I follow Austin Dean. He's one of the players I took a liking to because of his style of play. I'll check his stats. It was tough with him being gone the first half of the season."

Do you interact with the players?

"I try not to bother them too much. Growing up, when I was playing baseball, as a player you had to watch the game and pay attention to it. If I see them signing autographs for a long time I thank them for that."

What's the mix of old and new ushers?

"There are a few who've been here from when the Bragans owned the team for many years. There is a bunch like myself who came on with the new owner. We all work together. We're here to have a good time and help each other out."

Chase Foster, Account Executive

How hard is it to get people to have an event at the Baseball Grounds?

"The good thing about the marketing this year is we're getting a lot more call-ins. A lot of people like the idea of having their events here. It's more affordable than other events in the area. I might be personally biased but I think we put on a better all-around show than some of the other sporting events in town. It's a lot of fun. I'll call someone and they'll say they're not a baseball fan. I'm not selling baseball. You come to enjoy the rest of it. You might catch a couple of outs. I normally don't."

There are other things to do in the ballpark.

"Kidzone. Tiki corner. If you're a foodie there are a bunch of great options. Try the shrimp and grits one night and the burger pie the next. Have a sausage sandwich or a hot dog. There's something for everybody every night of the week. Sundays is kids and families. Friday night fireworks for the families, too. Thursday if you want to have a few beers and relax with your buddies it's the $1 beer night."

How does your job change when the team is on the road?

"That's more a nine to five when you're just in the office. We'll make calls until about one until our game day meeting, where we rundown what groups are in the building, what promotions we're doing, and anything else necessary. What groups will be in the building with a table and where. After that it is lunch and then everyone has a game day responsibility so you check in on that. I go check in

the kid's zone. During the week there are always people from groups calling in to do add-ons and last-minute changes to an event."

How far in advance are you looking at groups?

"We have a big board in our office that shows all the dates and open slots. Our job is to ask the right questions to see what someone with a potential event needs. I need to figure out how many employees they have. How many they want to bring out. Do they want to do just tickets? Do they want to add food? You have to find out their budget. See if they want privacy or shared picnic space. Privacy means up on one of the sky decks. With food you need to find out what options they're looking for. Traditional hot dogs and hamburgers or a few more things. Then what date they're looking for. Is it a weekday or a weekend you're looking for? Find out if it has to be a certain day of the week. Then we can look at the available dates and present some options for the event."

How many different people are doing that job?

"When you work in minor league baseball, everyone is expected to sell. In our office we had Clayton, who'll be replaced at some point. Then we have Taylor Boyle and James Abbatinozzi. Usually four as well as Theresa Viets, who is the military liaison, too. Plus Corey Marnik, the Director of Ticket Operations. Peter Ercey is the Box Office Manager. Brian DeLettre, the Creative Services Manager. Everyone in the office is expected to sell. The main priority is to put butts in the seats. If no one is coming to watch the games we don't have a reason to be here or have jobs. Plus, the players play better when there's a big crowd. It goes for the advertisers

in the stadium, too. If no one is here to see and read their signs they have no reason to do business with us. Bigger crowds mean more advertisers, which allows us to grow the brand and get more fans into the stadium and enjoy the game. Ticket sales are what drive the whole operation."

What is the goal with ticket sales?

"Groups drive attendance. That's how you fill the stadium. Ticket sales' driving the engine is common knowledge. The way to do that is to book groups. The easy way to pack the stadium is with groups. As far as season tickets: it's another important part. Its guaranteed revenue. To have those people committed is great for business. Plus, it's a loyal fan base. There's a reason they spent money for more than one game. They're fans. We also work with businesses to get them to purchase several seats, like your wife does. They use them to reward employees and use for clients. Jacksonville is a tough market. We like to educate our fan base. There used to be a large part of the crowd who'd show up five minutes before the game, stand in line at the box office and get their ticket. We can't do that anymore because of groups and season ticket holders. The goal is to let fans know, if they want to get their favorite spot, they should order ahead of time with a package. Purchase a plan. I look at the fans that have season ticket plans or other packages not just as clients but as friends. I want to know what's going on in their lives. I'll help out anyone with requests and ideas."

So for you it isn't just selling a bunch of group and season ticket plans and moving on to the next one.

"For me, the service after the sale is the most important part. It's one thing to collect the money and thank them, but if I don't follow through with what I promise, it doesn't mean anything. Harold Craw said it before: under-promise, over-deliver. That's the school I came from. In our training literature we talk about the wow factor. We want you to leave the game talking about us. For me personally it's always been my philosophy. Go over the top and above and beyond. It's what a lot of people do here, which is great. I want to make sure my clients are having a good time. They'll speak highly of me and the team. I'm the face for the organization when I deal with people. I'm always representing the Jumbo Shrimp in public. The easiest way to continue to generate revenue is making sure people have a good experience so they want to renew. It makes my job easier, too. I'm not calling new people all the time. I count on these people to come back. Then I get to see my friends again next season. They'll speak highly of us in the community. Word of mouth sells tickets, too. The best publicity is free publicity. During the game I try to visit every client at some point if possible. I keep up with people who've done events with us if I haven't seen them for awhile. Make sure everything is still great with them and if they want to come back for another event."

Andrea Williams, Director of Community Relations

What does your title mean?

"My job is to manage all relationships with nonprofits. I also handle events outside of the ballpark. Any appearances we may do like mascot, player, speaking engagements. I also do the donation for the team. Anytime anybody is looking for a donation I handle that. I also do all of our relationships with the schools. Any in-game programming we might do. And other duties assigned."

What is your day to day?

"I do make and take a lot of calls each day but it's usually on the go on my phone. Each day could be a variety of things. I also run guest services on game day, so I do the staffing in there. The 50/50 raffle seller is under me so I have to manage that, too."

How long have you been in this position?

"I came with the new ownership. When Ken Babby purchased the team and hired Harold Craw, Harold hired me."

Once the season ends, how does your job change?

"I'm also a member of the sales team. I also work on corporate sales. That's the start of our sales season. I'll transition into that and working on programming for the following year."

How early do you start looking at next year?

"June. I give it a couple of months to get integrated into the season. Once June comes I'm already looking at next year."

What are some of the fun things for you being part of the Jumbo Shrimp?

"I have a blast. I think I have one of the best jobs. I really get to market our brand outside of these doors. Every day. I might do a player appearance one day or be in khaki shorts and t-shirt with Scampi. I might be in a suit with the owner at an event. It varies and I get to tap into all the fun things people get to do."

Is the community coming to you or are you making it happen?

"We have some strategic partnerships. Like with the school district. We love working with children. A lot of the partnerships have come to us. We're extremely blessed in that nature. People want us involved in their events and their programming."

When the name change happened, how did that affect your job?

"I am one of the first lines of defense outside of these walls. Any event I went to, any programming, it was always the question. What are you guys doing over there? Why'd you change the name? Now it's more of how did you guys figure this out. Congratulations on your success. We do deem this year successful. They want to know what the next move is."

It was a lot of fun spending some time with the office staff.

The great part about the Jumbo Shrimp staff is you can run into most of them on the concourse during the game and they'll take the time to chat with you.

Let them know what a great job they're doing.

Chapter 37: August 4 - 8. Home vs. Birmingham Barons

August 4th

This was the last game for Clayton Edwards working with the Jumbo Shrimp. He was off to Illinois and his next adventure. When we got to the ballpark and started heading to our seats we stopped because it looked like someone was sitting in our spots. There were two full Diet Cokes in souvenir cups in our cup holders.

With a card from Clayton, who'd given us a going-away present. We're going to miss seeing him at every game and talking with him.

We'd taken him and his girlfriend to dinner a few nights ago and had a great time.

Our new account rep, Chase, came over. Proper introductions were done and I tried to con him into thinking taking over for Clayton meant he had to buy us drinks every game. It did not work.

Yuengling Guy was at this game. I haven't mentioned him before but he's been a fixture all season, sitting up in the front row right behind the Jumbo Shrimp dugout. He's a weekender, meaning he has these seats Friday and Saturday games.

The first thing he does once he's settled is buy a beer. But not just any beer. He has to have a Yuengling. He'll shake off a Bud or anything else like he's been given the wrong sign from his catcher.

Like I said, my wife and I like to watch the crowd. Yuengling Guy is funny. He makes faces at the players and he's always three seconds behind when the crowd does the wave, which makes everyone laugh.

You have to be there to really enjoy and understand it, I guess. See what you're missing?

Starter Matt Tomshaw got his tenth win of the season in a 7-2 victory in front of 6,634 fans on a Friday night. He gave up eight hits and two walks with seven strikeouts in six strong innings.

Jeff Kinley, Tyler Kinley and Severino Gonzalez pitched the last three innings without any problem to complete the win.

Kyle Barrett had two hits and scored three runs, and it was his 24th birthday, too.

In the eighth inning Cam Maron and Dustin Geiger hit back-to-back home runs.

Second baseman Alex Yarbrough went 2-for-4 with a run scored.

I asked Alex about his season and his second half.

How would you describe your season so far?

"It's been alright. Definitely been some ups and downs as far as having success. I've enjoyed my first year with the Marlins organization. I enjoyed playing with a lot of these guys I've never met before. Didn't know them five months ago and now I'm with them every day. It's been fun. Having some success as a

team helps a lot. We've had a good second half and looking forward to the playoffs now."

You got off to a slow start in the first half. What changed in the second half?

"I think it was putting all facets together. Early on we lost seven or eight in a row. A lot of nights it was because we weren't hitting. Our pitchers were throwing really well but we weren't scoring runs to back them up. One night we'd put up six or seven runs and it was the only game in the series the other team was hitting. In the second half, with the runs we've gone on, it's been the ability to protect leads. It's been huge. Especially our bullpen. The six game sweep against Birmingham and then almost shutting out Biloxi in the doubleheader. We've come together as a team."

August 5th

Starter Trevor Richards drew the short straw tonight, going against Barons righty Michael Kopech, one of the top prospects for the White Sox. I've been following Kopech because he was a top Red Sox prospect before being traded over in the Chris Sale swap.

Richards struck out seven in five innings but Kopech sat down eleven in seven innings and got the 2-1 win before 7,231 fans on a Saturday at the Baseball Grounds.

Braxton Lee went 2-for-3 and is still hitting .319 this late in the season. If he can keep it up he'll end up being the batting champion.

Former Jacksonville Jaguars quarterback Mark Brunnell threw out one of the ceremonial first pitches before the game started and got a nice hand from the crowd.

August 6th

The Jumbo Shrimp played with Aquaman jerseys, which were auctioned off to benefit Baptist Health Foundation and Wolfson Children's Hospital. My wife bid on a couple of them but lost to a higher bidder, which meant more money for the charity. So it was a win, although having a Braxton Lee or Austin Dean jersey hanging up in my Red Sox Room would've been sweet.

This was also the game I've been waiting for from the Jumbo Shrimp, with their bats coming alive. They scored twelve runs on thirteen hits in front of 2,813 fans.

The Jumbo Shrimp hit four home runs: two by Taylor Ard, who now has ten; Dustin Geiger hit his fourth and John Norwood connected for his sixteenth.

Austin Dean went 4-for-4 with a walk, had two RBI's and scored three runs. He had two doubles and a triple, too. He missed hitting for the cycle by a homer.

Lefty Dillon Peters (now 3-2) got the win, going five innings and giving up three runs.

August 7th

Luckily the Jumbo Shrimp only needed three runs to win tonight as the pitching held the Barons to 2 runs. Starter Joe Gunkel went 6 ⅓ innings, giving up one run and scattering nine hits. The bullpen took over and preserved the win as Esmerling De La Rosa, Tyler Kinley and Clayton Mortensen (who got his fifth save) finished the game.

Catcher Cam Maron went 2-for-4 with a double and an RBI.

I'm seeing them looser on the field and between innings, playing around and just having some fun out there. It's a good vibe in the stadium I hope continues.

August 8th

What was supposed to be a unique promotion ended in a wash-out. Luckily, I had the privilege of sitting in the radio booth with Roger Hoover and Marco LaNave, who showed me what they did when there was a rain delay.

They talked sports.

Everything from favorite baseball games to college football, volleyball and broadcasting in general. The pair takes their jobs very seriously but likes to have fun.

"I hope this game gets played. There was a lot of work put into this night," Marco said, watching the rain hitting the tarp below on the field.

It was supposed to be Silent Movie night. Jacksonville was a vital city for the silent film industry in the early twentieth century. The only remaining silent film studio and museum, Noram Studios, had partnered with the Jumbo Shrimp for this unique experience.

There would be no PA announcements. No recorded messages.

The video board would be black and white. Live music like you'd find in the original silent movies would be played.

And then the rains came and never stopped, until the game was finally called.

Not before I got to chat more with Roger, though.

With the trading deadline passing without the Marlins doing much of anything, how does your focus change?

"I always like to have a good working knowledge of what's going on within the organization. I keep abreast of what's going on in baseball as a whole, too. Whenever teams in our league make moves. It could impact who we'll see the next time we play them. How a certain series may go. It isn't something I talk to the players much about. It's mainly for my own personal knowledge."

What's the feel when they have to release a guy?

"It is part of the business everyone understands. It's never a good day when something like that happens. For me at least I'm pretty far from it. All of that is between the manager and coaches and the player. I don't really see a lot of the emotions of that. As someone who updates the roster, the Marlins send me everything once it's official. Whenever I get it in

my email I can alert the Jacksonville media. Put it on Twitter, things like that. It's a tough part of the business but I think all these players understand. It might be after a seven year minor league career. Maybe they never made it past Double-A. It may come after a twenty-year career in the majors for a ten-time All-Star. That day's going to come. Guys at the Double-A level have seen it come to a lot of their friends at a lower level. When it wasn't expected. I think they're always appreciative of the spot they're in. You try to stay as positive as you can. Joe Gunkel is a good example. He's been pitching great this year. Yet he was taken off the 40-Man roster for the Orioles. Taken off the Dodgers 40-Man, too. Picked up by the Marlins and taken off their 40-Man. Being in Double-A and finding his spot. Learning to adjust and have a great season despite those setbacks."

Do you understand a DFA move as it happens?

"I do. It's because of a need somewhere else. One of the 40-Man roster spots or somewhere else. It's all about helping the Marlins. What we're trying to do here in Jacksonville is help the Marlins win in Miami. It's not always about whether or not the Jumbo Shrimp are winning ballgames or what the organization needs to do to make that happen. It trickles down, too. Every move that happens on the Major League level will eventually affect every level below it."

How often are you getting the Marlins involved in the team as far as players are concerned?

"It's daily. They get very detailed reports from our manager. The pitching and hitting coaches. All about how the game went. There's video shot in every

single ballpark. We have a video coordinator who gets video just for our team. Anybody in the Marlins front office who wants it has access. Plus the games on MiLB.com which I know they're watching. I was in Miami during the All-Star Break and remember running into the GM one time and he's watching the Greensboro game on his iPad as he's watching the big league club, too. It's that important to them. They're constantly thinking about what's next. Whether or not to keep a guy at a certain level and for how long. Sometimes you have a game plan out of spring training for a certain guy. Other players you have to move around."

What about winning?

"They want the team to win. Anyone in baseball will tell you development is enhanced by winning. They want us to win and have a competitive team. That's at every level in the organization. But it's also about making sure these guys are ready to play and handle themselves at every level."

Braxton Lee comes over in the trade. Is any of that trade because of you seeing him playing in this league already?

"I think it influences it some. Our coaches will always have a report on different players they see. They work as scouts on their own level. Not nearly as detailed as a pro scout but they're always willing to point out the opposition they like. Every organization also has a list of ten or fifteen players from every other organization they like. If a trade were to come up they might already have a few names they want to deal for. A few years ago Justin Bour, who played for the Tennessee Smokies and was a Cubs first-base

prospect, was blocked ahead of him in the Major Leagues at the position. Anthony Rizzo is there. They also had another player in Triple-A blocking his path, too. The Cubs really didn't have a need for him so they didn't protect him on the 40-Man roster. The Rule 5 Draft comes around and Bour had played so well against the Suns and there were glowing reports from our manager. The Marlins picked him right up. He's been a big league starter ever since."

Are guys looking at the depth chart and wondering if they'll be able to move up in this organization?

"I think it's only natural. They also know if they continue to do good things they'll be in the major leagues anyway, whether it's Miami or somewhere else. The better they play the better their value to maybe another club with a need. The Marlins want these players to do very well. They might be a potential trade piece in the future so the Marlins can strengthen a weak position on the team. There are scouts from every team seeing these players all year long."

With the rain not letting up it was time to close up and go home. Tomorrow was a rare day off for the Jumbo Shrimp and I'm sure the players were eager to get changed and head out.

Righty Severino Gonzalez was promoted to New Orleans.

It was also my wife's birthday today. I guess she does really love baseball now, giving up her night to see a game that never materialized. She never got to see her birthday flashed on the board, either.

Don't worry, though. She had fun today. I swear.

Chapter 38: August 10 - 14. Home vs. Mississippi Braves

August 10th

Starter Chris Mazza went six innings with nine strikeouts, only giving up one run and was in line for the win until the bullpen let the game get away from them, giving up seven runs in the last two innings and taking a loss, 8-3. 5,007 were enjoying a great pitching performance until then.

Esmerling De La Rosa pitched a perfect seventh inning but then Tyler Kinley came in and gave up five straight hits and four runs without recording an out. Jeff Kinley relieved him and allowed three more runs in the last two innings.

The Jumbo Shrimp only had six hits, two of them by second baseman KC Serna.

My wife and I also got to add two more players to our sponsorship, with pitchers Trevor Richards and Jose Quijada getting travel snacks and drinks when the team went on their next road trip.

The team released righty Patrick Johnson.

August 11th

Matt Tomshaw got his eleventh victory and a 2-0 win in front of 6,485 fans on Red Shirt Friday who saw a great game and then fireworks afterwards.

Lefty Tomshaw went seven scoreless innings, scattering five hits and two walks while striking out five. Clayton Mortensen pitched the last two innings, only allowing two walks while striking out five for his sixth save of the year.

A home run by Austin Dean in the first inning, his third, and a Braxton Lee RBI was all the scoring the team needed.

M-Braves pitcher Mike Soroka went six innings but gave up both runs for the loss. His ERA is 2.70, tops in the Southern League. I'm telling you, this guy is going to be special for Atlanta along with Ronald Acuna, who's quickly moved up to Triple-A after running through the pitching in every stop along the way.

Righty Ryan Beckman was promoted from Jupiter to Jacksonville.

August 12th

The first thousand fans through the gate received a Jumbo Shrimp bowling shirt courtesy of Swisher International. They also received another Jumbo Shrimp win.

6,360 fans got a 5-2 Jumbo Shrimp win on a Saturday night.

Starter Trevor Richards went six innings, only giving up one hit and two walks while striking out eight for the win. He's now 4-4 on the season. Maybe the thought of us packing him chips and bottles of water for his next road trip had gotten him excited?

Neither team scored until the sixth inning. With two men on, first baseman Taylor Ard hit his eleventh home run of the season, a three-run shot.

Left fielder Austin Dean went 3-for-5 and right fielder John Norwood went 2-for-3 with two walks.

Tyler Kinley pitched the last 1 ⅔ innings for his sixth save.

August 13th

On a rainy Sunday, 2,833 fans saw the Jumbo Shrimp win, 9-3. The Jumbo Shrimp wore Guy Harvey-designed jerseys that were auctioned off to benefit the Guy Harvey Ocean Foundation.

My wife bid on a couple but we didn't win them.

Besides the Jumbo Shrimp team, the winner for tonight was Dillon Peters (now 4-2), who went five innings of two-hit ball, giving up a single run while striking out four.

If not for an hour rain delay he could've gone deeper in the game. He's definitely in his groove now and looked at ease on the mound tonight. Another player with great upside.

Tyler Higgins came in and pitched two innings, giving up two runs on two hits in two innings before Clayton Mortensen and Esmerling De La Rosa both pitched a scoreless inning to close it out.

First baseman Taylor Ard hit his twelfth home run of the season. He's been on a power surge lately, making it hard for Dustin Geiger to get into games except to pinch hit or when there's a designated hitter while playing an American League team.

During the game another fan stopped in the aisle and smiled at me. At first I had no idea what he was looking at until he pointed at my hat. I was wearing my green Ballantine's beer hat, a company that hasn't existed since the early 1970's.

I wear it because there's history for my family. Remember my grandfather, also Armand but known as Carideo? He worked for Ballantine's brewery in Newark New Jersey. I still have a few items passed down to me like Ballantine's trays I make my antipasto on. I bought the hat online because it's part of my history.

The fan was excitedly talking about growing up in New Jersey and he remembered drinking Ballantine's and his entire family would drink it. It was great talking to him although when the game started up again Ken, the usher, had to remind him to have a seat.

After the game the booster club had a picnic for the players. My wife volunteered to get the players to sign a bat that would be auctioned off at some point, so I followed her around as she got the signatures. All of the players in attendance were very accommodating.

She especially wanted to talk to pitcher Matt Tomshaw because when he occasionally batted in a game his walk-up music was *Fat Bottom Girls* by Queen. When she asked him he smiled and said his former team would never let him play it so when he asked he thought for sure the Jumbo Shrimp would say no. They didn't have a problem with it and it got the fans singing along each time.

We also met John Norwood's mom, in town to see her son. It was fun seeing him interact with his mother, so respectful and quiet around her. He's an intense guy but he seemed so relaxed with her.

I had the chance to talk to John Norwood during the season.

Do you look ahead? Guys playing in Triple-A and on the Marlins?

"No. That's out of my control. I can only take care of my ability and effort. I bring it forth every day. You can't think about that because this game is tough. It has different ways of bringing you up and bringing you down. If you're worrying about the guys in front of you or coming up behind you it won't work out. People will tell you what could happen if this guy moves up or down or is traded or hurt or whatever, but you try to focus on you and getting wins. If you get on the field and give it everything the rest falls into place."

Any game day rituals?

"No. I just come to the field everyday and have a good time. Every day is a new day. Try not to dwell on the past. Just enjoy it. There aren't many people that can say they get to play baseball and do something they've always dreamed of."

What do you write in the dirt before each at-bat?

"My grandparent's initials. They're with me. P & G."

At home you get to pick your walk-up music. On the road they sometimes play horrible intros to shake you.

"I hear the type of music I like. You might not like the music I listen to. You don't listen when they do that stuff. I tune it out. Listen to my walk-up music in my head. Do my routine getting to the plate. That song will go off."

August 14th

The Jumbo Shrimp lost, 8-2, in front of 2,207 on a Monday night.

Starter Joe Gunkel went 5 ⅓ innings, giving up eight runs on ten hits. He struck out three and gave up three home runs to the M-Braves.

Relievers Ryan Beckman and Jeff Kinley pitched the rest of the game, giving up no more runs, but it was already too late.

Jacksonville only had six hits, with first baseman Taylor Ard going 2-for-4.

I was at the stadium early to do a few more interviews and chat with Noel Blaha about how the book was coming along. During the first few innings I had been invited into the broadcasting booth again to watch and listen to Roger Hoover and Marco LaNave.

These two make a great team and hopefully they'll be working together calling the Jumbo Shrimp games for many years to come.

Chapter 39: Darren Daulton and Don Baylor

On August 6th the baseball world lost Darren Daulton.

The next day we lost Don Baylor.

I was a fan of both players growing up. It's sad to see someone you followed for many years pass away, especially so young.

Catcher Darren Daulton played for the Phillies and Marlins in his career. He was just fifty-five years old. He'd been battling brain cancer for the last four years.

For the first few years of his career he was a backup, joining the Phillies in 1983. In 1989 he got his chance to start and made the most of it, getting a spot on the All-Star team three times.

His nickname was Dutch. He was a key member of the 1993 Phillies team that went to the World Series. He played fourteen years in Philadelphia. He became a team leader and was loved by the fans.

In July of 1997 he was traded to the Florida Marlins. By this point in his career his knees were shot, yet he never quit. He played outfield for the Phillies in 1997 and then first base and as a pinch hitter for the Marlins, who stunned the world by winning the World Series.

Dutch retired after the World Series.

An ex of mine was a big Phillies fan and only because of two things: her father had season tickets to the games and she thought Darren Daulton was hot. Most women thought he was a good looking guy.

His first wife was Lynne Austin, a former *Playboy* Playmate. I remember hearing a story about how annoyed he was after they'd gotten divorced because a billboard with her picture was in the outfield at one of the stadiums and his teammates would make comments about it to bust his chops. Dutch took it in stride and during batting practice kept trying to hit the billboard.

I would go to many Phillies games in the mid-nineties to see them play. It was an easy drive from New Jersey and then we'd head over to Pat's or Geno's for a real Philly cheesesteak sandwich before the drive home.

When I was starting to get back into collecting baseball cards again I would always look for his rookie card, his 1985 Fleer Update card #U-33. At one point it was worth about ten bucks. Today they might be worth about two. I still have a framed picture of him in a box in one of my closets, too.

The Phillies came the closest to being a favorite team besides the Red Sox back then, because of players like Daulton, John Kruk and Lenny Dykstra. Rough and tumble players who might not do it pretty but they did it well.

I guess Daulton was pretty… Dutch will be missed.

Don Baylor did play for my Red Sox and was a feared slugger.

He passed away at sixty-eight years old battling multiple myeloma. Even though he only played for the Red Sox from 1986 to 1987, he was one of my favorite players.

Baylor started his career with the Baltimore Orioles from 1970 to 1975. He was traded to the Oakland Athletics as part of a six-man swap that included Reggie Jackson.

In 1977 he signed with the California Angels and played with them until 1982, and then played for the Yankees from 1983 to 1985. In 1986 he was traded to the Red Sox for Mike Easler. He was part of the Red Sox team that lost to the Mets in the World Series… which I still don't want to talk about.

In 1987 he got luckier, winning a World Series ring while playing for the Minnesota Twins. In 1988, his last year as a player, he went back to the World Series, this time with the Oakland Athletics.

From 1993 until 1998 he was manager of the expansion Colorado Rockies. He also managed the Chicago Cubs from 2000 to 2002. He spent the rest of his baseball career as either a hitting coach or bench coach for various organizations.

Don Baylor was always a larger-than-life character to me. One of those throwback 1970's players still around into the 1980's and beyond. He played left field and first base but I knew him as a feared designated hitter that had some big power years.

He was on the Red Sox during a couple of their homer-or-strikeout teams, a lineup filled with sluggers. He led the team with 31 home runs in 1986. Guys like Dwight Evans (26), Jim Rice (20) and Bill Buckner (18) were right behind him.

I followed his career even when he wasn't on the Red Sox and I rooted for the Twins in 1987 (when my team was out) because of Baylor.

Dutch and Don were two great players that helped shape my childhood as a baseball fan and I'll never forget the exciting moments they gave me.

Chapter 40: August 16 - 20. Away vs. Mobile BayBears

August 16th

We're starting to get down to the end of the season. Four series left. Two home. Two away. If the Jumbo Shrimp want to reach the playoffs they need to turn it on. They've been playing much better and looser lately.

They got off to an excellent start tonight, defeating the BayBears 3-2.

Starter Chris Mazza got the win with seven innings of two-run, five-hit ball. He struck out two. Daniel Schlereth, just back from New Orleans, got his third save with two scoreless innings to close it out.

Center fielder Braxton Lee went 1-for-4 with a run. His average is .315 and if he can keep up the pace he has a great chance of winning the Southern League batting title this year.

The win put them in first place, a half game in front of both the BayBears and Shuckers.

With Daniel Schlereth coming down pitcher Clayton Mortensen was moved up to New Orleans.

August 17th

It took ten innings but the Jumbo Shrimp won again, 6-2. With the score tied at two apiece the Jumbo Shrimp bats came alive in the top of the tenth.

After David Vidal and pinch hitter Dustin Geiger walked, Braxton Lee singled to knock Vidal in. John Norwood doubled to bring in Geiger. Taylor Ard doubled to bring in Lee and Norwood.

Esmerling De La Rosa pitched a scoreless bottom of the tenth to preserve the win. With the win the Jumbo Shrimp lead the South Division by a half game over the Shuckers and a full game over the BayBears.

August 18th

A 10-4 loss for the Jumbo Shrimp. Starter Trevor Richards allowed five runs on five hits with two walks. He only pitched ⅔ of an inning before he was pulled. The bullpen didn't fare much better, giving up five more runs on eight hits.

Third baseman David Vidal went 3-for-4 with two doubles and scored twice.

The Jumbo Shrimp are still in first place but only a half a game ahead of the BayBears and Shuckers.

August 19th

Starter Dillon Peters got his third straight win with six innings of two-hit ball. He walked two and struck out five. The 5-2 win kept them in first place and they have already clinched a rare road series win.

John Norwood hit his seventeenth homer of the season. Braxton Lee went 2-for-3 to raise his average to .325.

I had talked to Randy Ready about the team and as the season was winding down I knew we were seeing something special.

They seem looser now. What changed for them?

"I think you can attribute it to a couple of things. First, we have a lot of guys playing Double-A baseball for the first time. You have to get used to the speed of the game. What it entails day in and day out. Second, it's the chemistry. On good clubs players police players. That chemistry has to evolve when you have championship seasons. Those don't come around as often as we'd like them to. With that understanding, these guys have come together and I'm very proud of them. The chemistry within, internally, has come together. From a fan experience you can see them having fun. All the pieces are coming together at once at the right time," Randy said with a smile.

What kind of push do you as manager get from the Marlins organization about playing certain guys, and not just the rehab ones?

"There are no scholarships in this game. If you're playing well the manager is more likely to write your name in the lineup. The numbers will reflect that. Obviously, we still have priority guys. When we come out of spring training we know the guys probably getting the majority of playing time. But there are always diamonds in the rough. It's

always an opportunity for players to get themselves more playing time when they contribute. Keeping all that in mind, it still takes twenty-five guys. We've had promotions, we've had movement, guys we've demoted. There's always a chance we'll send a guy to the Marlins this year when rosters expand. That's the business we're in. As far as player development we keep all that in perspective. I really like what's happened this year."

What about a guy coming down for a rehab assignment?

"They're here to get their work in. When they arrive they need to play a certain amount of innings to start building themselves back up, either with playing a full game or a certain number of pitches. It comes from above. There's a plan set out ahead of time. They might need to play five innings. Three at-bats. A certain number of innings pitched. They're here to get back on their feet so they can go back up and contribute at the Major League level."

August 20th

Starter Joe Gunkel (now 4-9) took the loss in a 9-3 game. He pitched five innings but gave up five runs on nine hits. Relievers Jeff Kinley and Ryan Beckman each gave up two runs as well.

Third baseman David Vidal hit his ninth home run of the season.

The Jumbo Shrimp head back to Jacksonville still in first place with only fifteen games left to play.

Chapter 41: August 21 - 25. Home vs. Birmingham Barons

August 21st

A 4-1 win in front of 1,641 fans on a Monday night kept the Jumbo Shrimp in the lead for the South Division winner, with starter Chris Mazza going 7 ⅓ innings and only giving up one run on five hits.

Esmerling De La Rosa finished the eighth inning with two strikeouts and Tyler Kinley struck out the side in the ninth for his seventh save of the season.

Braxton Lee, Austin Dean and KC Serna all doubled in the win.

Lefty Daniel Schlereth was promoted to New Orleans and lefty Miguel Del Pozo promoted to Jacksonville from Jupiter.

August 22nd

Doubleheader Tuesday. Two For Tuesday?

In game one starter Matt Tomshaw pitched his first complete game of the year. He's now (12-6) on the season. He allowed eight hits and one walk, striking out five while giving up three runs in the 4-3 win, which the Jumbo Shrimp managed with three runs in the bottom of the seventh inning to win. Since it was a doubleheader day, both games would be seven innings.

In the seventh, down 3-1, catcher Cam Maron hit a triple and was knocked in by second baseman KC Serna. Shortstop Cleuluis Rondon made his Jumbo Shrimp debut (against his former team) and had a sacrifice fly, bringing in KC Serna and tying the game.

Austin Dean singled to bring in the winning run.

Would game two be as exciting?

Tyler Higgins, usually a reliever, was pressed into starting duty because of the extra game. He went 4 ⅓ innings with seven strikeouts. He gave up two runs and had the lead when he left, but Miguel Del Pozo couldn't record an out, giving up the tying run on two hits and a walk. Andy Beltre came in and pitched 1 ⅔ scoreless innings and got the win. Righty Esmerling De La Rosa pitched a scoreless seventh for his first save.

So, how did they do it this time? David Vidal hit his tenth home run of the season, knocking in two runs for a 5-3 victory in the sixth inning.

Two much-needed wins this close to the end of the season. You can see these guys know they have a chance to win every night now.

The Jumbo Shrimp placed shortstop Chris Diaz on the 7-Day DL with a dislocated shoulder, which is why Cleuluis Rondon was promoted from Jupiter and in the game.

August 23rd

Three pitchers combined on a 5-0 shutout and the Jumbo Shrimp won their fourth straight game in front of 3,197 fans at the Baseball Grounds.

Trevor Richards started and Jeff Kinley and Tyler Kinley added to the scoreless streak.

This was also the seventh straight home series they've won and they kept their two-game lead over the BayBears in the South Division.

Catcher Cam Maron went 2-for-4 and knocked in three runs.

August 24th

The games were rained out, meaning they'll have to play a doubleheader tomorrow in order to get every game in this season so far. Hopefully this isn't a momentum shifter for the Jumbo Shrimp, who look unstoppable.

They lead by two games with twelve left to play.

Pitcher Daniel Schlereth was brought down from New Orleans and pitcher Jose Quijada came up from Jupiter.

August 25th

Another doubleheader because of postponed games in the past. Two seven-inning games might be cause for concern when the team is playing every game that's meaningful and hopefully getting closer to a playoff berth.

Spoiler alert: two more wins in front of 7,944 fans on a Friday night put the Jumbo Shrimp ahead by three games in the South Division and a six-game sweep of the Barons.

In game one starter Dillon Peters pitched 6 ⅔ innings without giving up a run. He's now 6-2 on the season and the internet rumor floating around this week is he'll be called up to the Marlins when rosters expand on September 1st.

Daniel Schlereth struck out the last batter and picked up his fourth save in the 4-0 win.

The Jumbo Shrimp scored all four runs in the fourth inning. Shortstop Cleuluis Rondon hit a double, center fielder Braxton Lee singled, left fielder Austin Dean had an RBI single followed by an RBI double for right fielder John Norwood. Second baseman KC Serna hit an RBI single. Designated hitter Kyle Barrett got another RBI for the Jumbo Shrimp with a groundout.

In game two's win starter Joe Gunkel went 5 ⅓ innings, giving up three runs on ten hits with two strikeouts. Esmerling De La Rosa picked up his second save of the season in the 5-3 win.

Other highlights included John Norwood going 3-for-4 with three RBI. KC Serna went 2-for-3.

The Jumbo Shrimp will be on the road against Biloxi and then return home for the season-ending series against Pensacola, who look to be their opponents in the playoffs.

But first they need to keep winning so they can get there. Right?

Chapter 42: Marlins Sold?

Just in case I haven't said it enough in this book so far… I am not a Yankees fan. I do not like them. Never will. I will root against them no matter who they are playing. I will not watch a World Series if they are in it.

Yet… I do have respect for certain players that have never worn a Red Sox jersey. I've talked about a few of them so far like Darren Daulton and Cal Ripken Jr.

I'd add Derek Jeter to this list. He was never arrogant. He never showed up anyone and he never added to the rivalry by doing anything over the top. The guy just went out there and beat you with his glove and bat. I respect him for it.

Venture Capitalist Bruce Sherman was buying the Miami Marlins for a reported $1.17 billion and his partner and who would become the head of baseball operations was Jeter.

It is rumored Michael Jordan, who owns the Charlotte Hornets of the NBA is also involved in a small capacity.

As of right now this is all unsubstantiated rumors. *The Miami Herald*'s anonymous source leaked the sale. If true, it would get Jeffrey Loria out of baseball. I think it's a good thing.

What would it mean to the franchise besides a different owner or owner group?

Hopefully this will lead to a better game plan for the Marlins.

While I love the Jumbo Shrimp and quite a few players in the minor league system I know they need help. The organization from top to bottom is weak from a prospect standpoint.

While the Marlins have some great players on their roster like Giancarlo Stanton, Christian Yelich, Dee Gordon and JT Realmuto and a few others, there isn't much to look forward to in the farm system right now.

While several Jumbo Shrimp players should eventually reach the Marlins, they lack pitching depth and players who can step into all nine positions if needed.

Unlike other organizations, they aren't a threat with prospects and the future.

My hope would be for the team to make some changes on the field. Nothing major. Just getting rid of some fringe players and getting a decent package of prospects back for them.

You have to start rebuilding the Marlins from the bottom up. Better drafts. Better international signings. Working on the guys on the farm to get them ready for the Marlins at some point.

I don't have the exact ranking but I know the Marlins are towards the bottom with their minor league system.

Do I think a fire-sale is inevitable? Yes. Loria has done it in the past so there is precedent. Unfortunately, looking at the payroll of the Marlins and the few wins they've gotten lately, I think something big is going to happen in Miami.

Now, on the fan side of things and especially when it comes to my favorites on the Jumbo Shrimp, I think it's a good thing.

There will be some big opportunities for position players like Brian Anderson, John Norwood, Austin Dean and Braxton Lee to get the call-up sooner than later.

Seeing players we rooted for in Jacksonville get to The Show is a great thing to look forward to.

Because of this season I'm now invested in what the Marlins are doing as well as the Red Sox.

If you'd told me two years ago I'd even care or know more than a handful of their players I would've laughed. Now I know their depth charts by position and I see a few Jumbo Shrimp players creeping up on the lists.

Very exciting.

Chapter 43: August 26 - 30. Away vs. Biloxi Shuckers

August 26th

A 7-6 win (their seventh straight victory) kept the Jumbo Shrimp in first place for the second half of the season. Their lead is three games with nine to play. They're also now 65-63 on the season after a lackluster first half.

Starter Chris Mazza pitched five innings, giving up five earned runs on eight hits and a walk while striking out three. When he left Biloxi was winning 6-3. Ryan Beckman came in and pitched a scoreless inning, followed by Andy Beltre and Tyler Kinley.

The Jumbo Shrimp came back in the seventh with a sacrifice fly by KC Serna and an RBI double by Taylor Ard to get it to within one run. Pinch hitter Kyle Barrett hit the first pitch he saw for a two-run RBI single to give them the lead.

With the Jumbo Shrimp relievers pitching so well it was the final scoring in the game. Beckman got the win (he's now 3-0) and Kinley got his eighth save.

Jacksonville got eleven hits in this game, including Cam Maron, who went 3-for-3 and John

Norwood, David Vidal and Taylor Ard with two hits apiece.

August 27th

The winning streak ended as the Jumbo Shrimp lost, 10-5 to the Shuckers.

Starter Matt Tomshaw went five innings, giving up four runs on seven hits.

Esmerling De La Rosa took the loss, blowing the save as he gave up four runs in ⅔ of an inning.

John Norwood hit his eighteenth home run of the season. He has a chance to hit twenty for the year, which would be impressive. Heck, eighteen is impressive.

Tomorrow is another day and another game.

August 28th

It was a 7-1 loss tonight but no need to panic… yet. I am, after all, a Red Sox fan. Despite recent World Series wins in my lifetime, I know it can all fall apart quickly.

Maybe by listening to the away games I'm a *mush* for the team.

After an hour rain delay the game began and it rained throughout most of the game but they needed to get this one in.

Starter Trevor Richards got the loss, giving up five runs (only two earned) on six hits with a walk and four strikeouts. He lasted five innings.

With seven games left in the season the Jumbo Shrimp still hold a three game lead over the BayBears and Shuckers.

Highlights included catcher Rodrigo Vigil batting in third baseman David Vidal, who doubled. Braxton Lee and KC Serna got the other two hits in the game.

Speaking of KC Serna, I got to talk to him during the season.

How is it working for a manager like Randy Ready, who's been to The Show?

"You definitely think about it when you work with a coach who's been in the Big Leagues, especially as long as he had. He's an interesting dude because he brings a different vibe to the manager's spot. Randy keeps things really loose. He likes to have a good time. When it's time to get down to business he's always the one to make sure you're putting the work in and doing what needs to be done and ready for the game. I definitely appreciate that about him."

Different vibe end of season?

"As a team we all started to click at the same time. It didn't hurt we were making a playoff push. It was good timing. I just think we finally found the right mesh of guys. The same guys were playing every day and we got rid of the guys who weren't holding their own or stopped playing, and it all clicked at the right time."

August 29th

The game was postponed due to rain. If they could've played this one they would've. Now it will be a doubleheader of two seven-inning games tomorrow.

In roster moves, righty James Needy was promoted from Jupiter and lefty Jeff Kinley was sent down to Jupiter.

August 30th

Two games and two wins for the Jumbo Shrimp. This is the way to roll into the playoffs, on a big winning streak.

The first game went 1-0 in eleven innings.

Righty James Needy made his Jumbo Shrimp debut and went six innings of scoreless ball, only giving up four hits and three walks while striking out six. Tyler Kinley pitched two scoreless innings in relief and then Daniel Schlereth pitched the last three innings to get his first win of the season without giving up a run.

The lone run came on a wild pitch, scoring Alex Yarbrough from third. He'd walked and gone to second when Braxton Lee was also walked. Austin Dean singled, putting Yarbrough at third.

In the second game starter Joe Gunkel went 6 ⅓ innings, giving up one run on four hits. He struck out five. He's now 6-9 on the season.

Biloxi had four errors in the game which led to at least one of the runs. John Norwood went 2-for-4 and Rodrigo Vigil 2-for-2.

With the doubleheader win, the Jumbo Shrimp can clinch their first playoffs since 2014 with a win over Pensacola to open their final homestand tomorrow.

How exciting!

Chapter 44: August 31 - September 4. Home vs. Pensacola Blue Wahoos

August 31st

The Jumbo Shrimp clinched the playoffs and won the game in dramatic fashion, breaking a 2-2 tie in the bottom of the eighth inning to win 5-2.

4,609 fans got to see the victory and the celebration that happened afterwards on the field.

Starter Chris Mazza went 6 ⅓ innings. He gave up two runs on six hits but didn't get the decision. That went to Miguel Del Pozo, who pitched 1 ⅔ scoreless innings for his first win. Esmerling De La Rosa pitched a scoreless ninth for his third save.

Right Fielder Jon Norwood hit his nineteenth home run off of Deck McGuire. I still think that is a cool baseball name.

Norwood also had a two-run triple to make it 5-2 after Austin Dean hit the go-ahead single for the lead.

It was an amazing night of baseball.

During the beginning of the game I talked with owner Ken Babby, who came to our seats and I followed him to a quiet tunnel to chat about the team. I didn't want to take up too much of his time because we both wanted to get back to the game. I will say once again what a generous owner he is and the great staff under him.

Pitcher Jeff Kinley was brought back up from Jupiter.

The Detroit Tigers traded pitcher Justin Verlander to the Houston Astros. I knew my dad would be calling me very early in the morning to vent about his team tossing in the towel in such a big way at the trading deadline.

September 1st

Starter Matt Tomshaw went seven innings and struck out seven, both season highs, while also tying the Southern League wins lead with thirteen. It was a 6-3 win for the Jumbo Shrimp in front of 5,744 fans on a Friday night who came for baseball and fireworks.

Left fielder Austin Dean hit his fourth home run of the season and first baseman Dustin Geiger hit his fifth.

It was announced before the game and spread throughout the stadium the Miami Marlins had called up two players when the rosters expanded from 25 to 40: Pitcher Dillon Peters, who would be starting tonight as well as Brian Anderson, who looked to get the start at third base.

Dillon Peters pitched seven shutout innings in his Major League debut but didn't get the win as veteran closer Brad Ziegler blew the game in the ninth.

Brian Anderson got his first Major League hit and had a couple of nice plays on defense.

As soon as the Jumbo Shrimp game was over we rushed home so I could watch the highlights and see Peters and Anderson in their Marlins uniforms.

I won't say I'm surprised by either player getting promoted but it is still an awesome thing to see, and I can't wait to see what they both do for the rest of the season and what 2018 brings for both of them.

And many more players in the future.

Austin Dean, who is very close to Brian Anderson and roomed with him during the season, had this to say about him.

"I'm super happy for him. A little upset we didn't get to finish the season together. But I was happy because when it was announced he was heading to Triple-A it meant he's one step closer to getting to the big leagues. Knowing he went to the Marlins and got to start in his first game and did well is awesome. He deserves every bit of it."

What about Austin and his career?

"Right now I just want to play the game. I'm not pushing to do anything spectacular. I just want to help the Shrimp win baseball games. Just do my job and help the team win games. It would be all I need."

When did he know he was ready to come back after the injury?

"As soon as I was 100% I was back. I want to play every day but I don't make lineups. Skip does. If he wants me in that day I'm ready to go. If he doesn't want me in I'm fine with it. That's baseball. You have to deal with it."

I believe if his season wasn't derailed in the beginning Austin Dean might've been a September call-up as well.

Dillon Peters had a great run with the Jumbo Shrimp and I wondered what pitching coach Storm Davis, a Jacksonville native who still lives here, thought.

A pitcher like Dillon Peters moves to the Marlins. Is it a great thing or just part of the job?

"I've been blessed. I've coached a lot of guys in the last seven years who've gotten there. I'm proud for him. He put in all the work. All I'm doing is giving him a little advice here and there. I don't even think of things like that. I'm just thrilled for him."

How is it coming home and working with the Jumbo Shrimp?

"It's been a good experience. This is obviously home for me. It has been on and off since 1968. I've coached in three different organizations. This has always been my winter address. This is the first year I've coached in Jacksonville with the Miami Marlins. I've coached in this ballpark before as a high school coach. I'm not a goal guy or expectations guy. I just go day to day. It's been a good group of kids to work with."

You've worked with some of these players already when you were coaching in New Orleans last year.

"We had Tomshaw occasionally. Tyler Kinley a little bit. I've seen a few of these guys last year but this was my first full year to see what this pitching staff can do."

What was your expectation coming into the season?

"I don't get into long-term things. I just think you look at it that way at this level. I'm looking for an

extra one percent. One percent better per month. Everyone has different things they need to get a little better at. It's why we're here in the minor leagues. For the most part it's been a good year along those lines. Guys have improved in whatever way they needed to. Some of them haven't been here very long. That's why you look more in short-term than long-term. It's inevitable that the roster is going to change over here and there. I have to deal with today's game. Every year as a player you try to get a little better at something."

You've had a great career in the major leagues. Do you talk about it with these players or ignore it and teach?

"I try not to shove that door in. I need to be asked in. I never play the Big League card. I think it comes off as condescending. I'm a quiet guy. Sometimes I might come off like that. I don't know. I don't mean it to be. The coaching part you've got to stay on top of it. If they have a question I do the best I can to help them. I try to give them the short-term and then the long-term answer to whatever issue they're dealing with."

September 2nd

The Blue Wahoos took this game, 3-1, in front of 4,175 fans on a Saturday night. It stopped the Jumbo Shrimp winning streak at eight games.

Starter Trevor Richards took the loss, going six innings while only giving up three runs (none of them earned) on five hits with seven strikeouts.

Miami Marlins first baseman Justin Bour, on a rehab assignment, played six innings.

Third baseman David Vidal went 2-for-4 with the only RBI for the Jumbo Shrimp.

September 3rd

It was a 2-1 win in front of 8,046 fans on Fan Appreciation on a Sunday night.

Starter Joe Gunkel looked strong, putting down the first fourteen batters he faced. A pair of runs in the sixth inning was the difference.

Rehabbing Justin Bour connected for a home run in his first at-bat. It was the only scoring for the Jumbo Shrimp.

September 4th

In the regular season finale the Jumbo Shrimp got the 5-1 win over the team they'll be facing in the playoffs.

Center fielder Braxton Lee went 2-for-4, both hits coming in his last two at-bats. With the .309 batting average he won the Southern League batting title.

Rehabbing Justin Bour also went 2-for-4 with two singles.

What an end to the season. I couldn't wait for the playoffs to begin, although it looked like Mother Nature was going to have a say in how the next few days turned out.

Chapter 45: Hurricane Irma

The worst-case scenario is upon us.

Besides Jacksonville currently in the path of Hurricane Irma, the baseball playoffs have been thrown into chaos.

Because of the impending weather, the Southern League has decided to cancel the championship series.

The division playoffs will decide co-winners of the Southern League title this year. Southern League president Lori Webb made the decision due to the safety of the players and the fans. With a probable evacuation and supply shortages in the near future, it didn't seem wise to go ahead with all of the games.

The winner of the Jumbo Shrimp and Blue Wahoos will be the South Division champion, while the Lookouts and Biscuits will decide the North Division.

Because of the incoming Hurricane, the series will be changed for the South. Game one and two is scheduled for Pensacola but now instead of game three, four and five being played in Jacksonville they will be moved, with game three staying in Pensacola but the Jumbo Shrimp as the home team. If games four and five are necessary they will be played in Biloxi.

Obviously I understand the decision but it bums me out. I was all excited to see playoff baseball, especially after following the team all year and being invested emotionally.

Being unable to see any of the games and then not having an actual Southern League championship is upsetting.

Don't get me wrong… I understand completely.

My wife and I start to look at the calendar. If they go to game four and maybe five we might head to Biloxi and get out of the path of Hurricane Irma.

Chapter 46: Playoffs September 6 - 8 Away vs. Pensacola Blue Wahoos

September 6th

Pensacola took the first game of the playoffs, 2-0.

Starter Chris Mazza took the tough loss, going seven innings while giving up one run on six hits. He struck out five.

Deck McGuire went eight scoreless innings to get the win for the Blue Yahoos.

The Jumbo Shrimp will get them tomorrow.

Lefty Jeff Kinley was assigned to Jupiter, swapped for righty Ben Meyer.

September 7th

Another loss, this time 6-3. Starter Matt Tomshaw took the loss, going seven innings and giving up three runs on seven hits. Ben Meyer, just called up from Jupiter, went two innings but gave up three runs on two hits and a walk.

Third baseman David Vidal hit a home run and knocked in two.

Pitcher Esmerling De La Rosa was placed on the 7-Day DL with shoulder inflammation. Pitcher Jeff Kinley was brought back up from Jupiter.

If the Jumbo Shrimp can win tomorrow we might get a room in Biloxi, especially since Hurricane Irma will hit Jacksonville and we'll lose power.

September 8th

The game went twelve innings but in the end the Jumbo Shrimp were on the short end, losing 5-4 and getting eliminated from the playoffs.

Jacksonville had nine hits but couldn't make a dent in the Blue Wahoos pitching.

The season is over.

Even though it wasn't the dream ending I envisioned for the team, just getting to the playoffs after an off first-half is amazing.

When I tell my wife they lost and there would be no games tomorrow and none until 2018, she sighs.

Then between hurricane preparations we talk about renewing our seats in Section 102 for next season.

Chapter 47: End of Season

Thanks to the name change, the management, on-field excitement and great baseball, the Baseball Grounds had the largest increase in attendance from last year to this year in Double-A.

It was a twenty-three percent increase in attendance and the largest in the ballparks history. 325,743 fans witnessed the first Jumbo Shrimp season.

As I said before, Braxton Lee won the Southern League batting title. His .03882 average beat out Chattanooga's Jonathan Rodriguez, who hit .30876. That is close.

Braxton also lead the league in hits with 147.

There were a lot of other positives out of Jacksonville, too.

Jumbo Shrimp General Manager Harold Craw won the 2017 Southern League Jimmy Bragan Executive of the Year and the Jumbo Shrimp were the winners of the 2017 Southern League Don Mincher Organization of the Year as well as the 2017 Southern League Promotion Trophy.

On the player's side, right-handed starter Trevor Richards was named the 2017 Miami Marlins Minor League Pitcher of the Year. He went 12-11 in 27 games (25 of them starts) with a 2.53 ERA, pitching for both Jupiter and Jacksonville. He set career highs in wins, innings pitched and strikeouts. He led the Marlins minor league system in ERA and strikeouts, with 158. This was his first full minor league season. He was a Florida State All-Star as well.

Pitcher Raudel Lazo signed with the Bowie Baysox (Double-A for the Baltimore Orioles) in early August after being out of baseball since being cut in May.

David Vidal was released after the season was over.

Hunter Adkins was released and went to Tampa Bay, playing on their Double-A and Triple-A teams.

Rojos del Aguila de Veracruz signed free agent RF Jeremias Pineda in July 2017.

Many players never got back to baseball after being released.

After the season, with the sweeping changes the new management group made, many star players were traded. In theory it will open up Major League spots for many players such as Braxton Lee, Austin Dean and John Norwood, not to mention the many prospects the Marlins traded for.

The 2018 Jacksonville Jumbo Shrimp might look like a completely new team, with most of the players new to the Southern League and the better players from this year in Triple-A or Miami.

I'll be rooting for all of them as I take my seat in Section 102, row J seat 1. Right next to my wife… once she gets back from buying us jumbo hot dogs, nachos in a souvenir helmet and a couple of Diet Cokes in a souvenir Jumbo Shrimp cups.

Armand Rosamilia is a New Jersey boy currently living in sunny Florida, where he writes when he's not sleeping. He's happily married to a woman who helps his career and is supportive, which is all he ever wanted in life...

He's written over 150 stories that are currently available, including horror, zombies, contemporary fiction, thrillers and more. His goal is to write a good story and not worry about genre labels.

He not only runs two successful podcasts...

Arm Cast: Dead Sexy Horror Podcast - interviewing fellow authors as well as filmmakers, musicians, etc.

The Mando Method Podcast with co-host Chuck Buda - talking about writing and publishing

But he owns the network they're on, too! Project Entertainment Network

He also loves to talk in third person... because he's really that cool.

You can find him at http://armandrosamilia.com for not only his latest releases but interviews and guest posts with other authors he likes!

and e-mail him to talk about zombies, baseball and Metal:

armandrosamilia@gmail.com

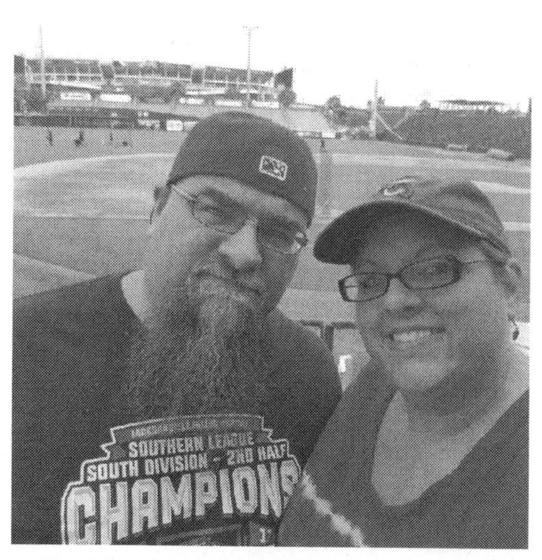
SOUTHERN LEAGUE
SOUTH DIVISION - 2ND HALF
CHAMPIONS

Check out his crime thriller series, too!

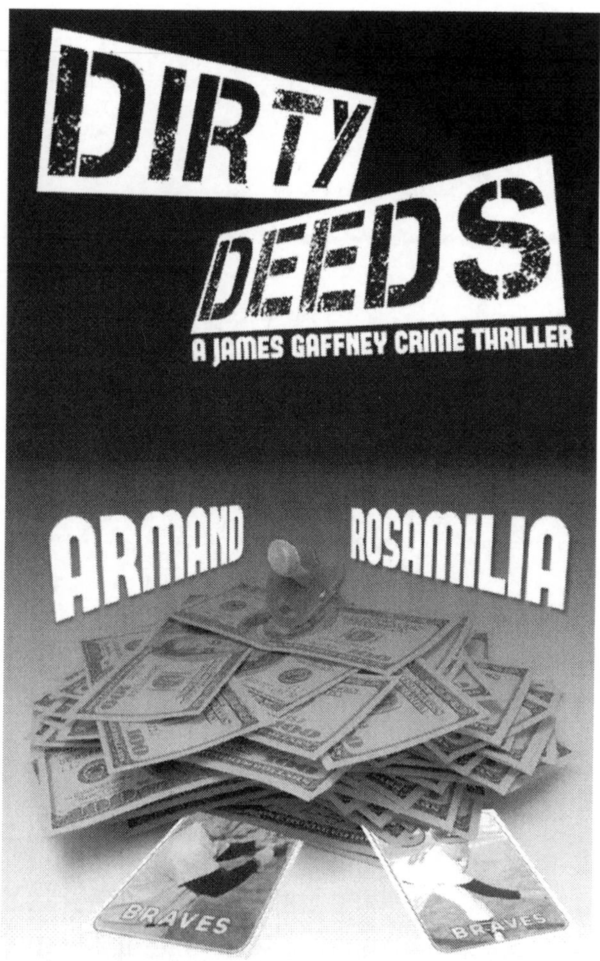